1

23.

14.

STUDIES IN FRENCH LITERATURE No. 12

General Editor
W. G. Moore

GIDE:
L'IMMORALISTE AND
LA PORTE ETROITE

by

J. C. DAVIES

Professor of French
University of New England, Australia

EDWARD ARNOLD
41 Maddox Street, London W.1.

© J. C. DAVIES 1968

First published 1968 by
Edward Arnold (Publishers) Ltd.,
41 Maddox Street, London W1R OAN
Reprinted 1971

Cloth edition ISBN: 0 7131 5293 1
Paper edition ISBN: 0 7131 5518 3

Reproduced and printed in Great Britain
by Latimer Trend & Co. Ltd., Whitstable

Contents

PAGE

INTRODUCTION   7

1. ORIGINS   10

2. TECHNIQUES   18
   The Classical Artist   18
   The First-Person Narrator   25
   Irony   31
   Style   40

3. STRUCTURE   52
   Structure and Symbolism   52
   (a) *Structure of Plot*   56
   (b) *Characters*   63
   (c) *Background*   69

4. AFFINITIES   71

SELECT BIBLIOGRAPHY   77

SUGGESTED APPROACHES TO GIDE   79

BRIEF CHRONOLOGY   80

*For Milla
and the children*

Introduction

The publication, in 1958, of the first joint edition of *L'Immoraliste* and *La Porte étroite*,[1] realised a project that would have found favour with André Gide himself. On many an occasion, in his correspondence, he stressed the complementary nature of these two *récits*, which, in his view, belonged together, just as they were conceived together. Coexisting and developing simultaneously in his mind, the two works depended on each other for their very existence, for "je n'aurais pu écrire l'*Immoraliste*, si je n'avais su que j'écrirais aussi la *Porte étroite*."[2] And, if one work appeared some seven years after the other, this, we are assured, was due to purely external factors and to the sheer physical impossibility of writing them together! Yet l'*Immoraliste* has for too long been neglected in favour of its twin, particularly as a text in schools and colleges. Furthermore, Alissa's ideal has been admired and Michel's conduct condemned, without due regard for the intentions of the author. It is only by examining these works together that we are able to put them both in their true perspective. It was partly to achieve this, and to restore a balance which has hitherto been too heavily tilted in one direction, that the present study was undertaken.

At the same time, these *récits* provide an excellent introduction to the work of Gide. They are entirely representative of the most interesting period of his evolution—that which covers the first twenty years of his literary career, a period marked by the most intense conflict between opposing tendencies in his nature. This conflict gives to the creative works of Gide's youth and early maturity the tension of an inner *angoisse* which largely disappears from the later works. We feel that Gide at this period is driven by an inner compulsion to write, that his books are the necessary, though bitter, expression of personal suffering and anguish. It would be quite misleading to discuss *in isolation* a single example of the works of this period, for each successive work is but a phase in a series of actions and reactions. Gide, at this time, is torn between two violently opposing ideals—a tortured quest for God,

[1] Published by *Le Club des Libraires de France*, 380 p.
[2] Letter to André Beaunier (12th July 1914).

7

amid a background of puritanical restraint and inhibition, on the one hand, and a frenzied lust for life and freedom on the other. *L'Immoraliste* and *La Porte étroite*, taken together and duly compared, present a more or less faithful image of the opposing forces at war in the mind of Gide at this troubled period of his life.

Complementary but forming a unity, like the two panels of a diptych, these works represent contrasting aspects of the same problem—one which was, indeed, the central problem of Gide's youth. Gide expressed it himself in the following terms: "la fin de l'homme est-elle Dieu, est-elle l'homme?"[1] In l'*Immoraliste*, the author took as his starting point the assumption that the end of man was, in fact, man, and showed the hero's attempt to discover his true personality and realise to the full his hidden potentialities. "Qu'est-ce que l'homme peut encore? Voilà ce qu'il m'importait de savoir."[2] But that man may increase, God must decrease, and *L'Immoraliste*, in three highly significant and symbolic episodes, shows the rejection of religion and a dependence on man alone. Gide's intentions are made clear by his statement during an interview on the French Radio, shortly before his death: "*(L'Immoraliste)* reprend le conflit de l'homme avec Dieu. Il grandit l'homme contre Dieu." *La Porte étroite* postulates the opposite point of view, assuming the all-powerfulness of God and the insignificance of Man. Alissa sacrifices man's claims to happiness in this world to a longed-for communion with God in the next world and places her whole trust in religion. "Malheur à l'homme qui met sa confiance dans l'homme."[3] The contrast between the two works is perhaps best illustrated by Alissa's own statement of her ideal, which becomes in effect an implicit condemnation of the attitude of Michel: "Ce qu'il faut chercher c'est une *exaltation* et non point une émancipation de la pensée. Celle-ci ne va pas sans un orgueil abominable. Mettre son ambition non à se révolter, mais à servir . . ."[4]

It is significant that both Michel and Alissa fail in their respective quests. Michel destroys both his wife and his own happiness. Alissa breaks her cousin's heart, and brings about her own death. This occurs

[1] Quoted by Lafille, *A. Gide Romancier*, p. 43.

[2] *L'Immoraliste*, p. 162. The edition of *L'Immoraliste* used is that published by the *Mercure de France* (1962).

[3] Quoted in *La Porte étroite*, p. 100. The edition of *La Porte étroite* used is that published by the *Mercure de France* (1961).

[4] *La Porte étroite*, p. 110.

because of the *excess* to which both protagonists carry their ideal, so that it becomes a dangerous obsession, almost a temporary insanity. It should, after all, be possible for reasonable people to reconcile a desire for self-realisation or a longing for God with the claims of a normal married life. But Alissa and Michel refuse to compromise or to accept any dilution of their ideal: Alissa is revolted by the idea of Juliette's "conventional" happiness and Michel is unwilling to submit to a static bourgeois existence with Marceline. Both are hopeless romantics yearning for the unattainable, but at the same time dangerous fanatics who are to serve as a warning. It is in this sense that Gide referred to *La Porte étroite* as "la critique d'une certaine tendance mystique" and to *L'Immoraliste* as "la critique d'une forme de l'individualisme", for his intention was to show that an excess of virtue or saintliness could be no less ruinous than an excess of independence and self-development. From this point of view, *L'Immoraliste* and *La Porte étroite* could be said to represent opposing swings of the same pendulum, the movement in one direction finding its counterpart, and its justification, in a corresponding movement to the other extreme.

Gide has continually stressed the fact that these books are in effect "des livres ironiques", and we have devoted a considerable portion of our study to examining Gide's technique of irony in the two *récits*. Not the least of these ironies is his attribution of typically human failings to these fanatics enamoured of the *inhumain*. They refuse the possibility of conventional human happiness, yet they remain attached, in spite of themselves, to a human being whom they love, and it is this attachment which is one of the reasons, if not the principal reason, for the failure of their quest. Alissa loves Jérôme, Michel loves Marceline, and a violent conflict is set up between their impossible ideal and an ordinary human being's need for love. The superhuman heroes become frail, ordinary mortals like ourselves. The purity of their ideal is further compromised by the mixed motives which the author assigns to them, not directly or explicitly, but by means of subtle hints and suggestions. Michel is engaged in a disinterested quest for self-realisation and self-understanding, but, beneath the surface, there is many a hint to suggest that egotism and the selfish pursuit of pleasure are equally strong incentives. The sublimity of Alissa's quest for God is similarly compromised by suspicions of an inordinate pride finding expression in self-sacrifice, and by suggestions even of a contrary motive—a basic fear of life, arising from strong sexual inhibitions, which causes her to seek refuge in

God. The purity of the original ideal is thus diluted, but we can at least warm to Alissa and Michel as human beings.

Irony forms a major element in the composition of both these *récits*, which, in addition to developing complementary themes, display considerable similarity of technique. Devices common to both works, such as the use of irony and the technique of the first person narrator, will be analysed in a later chapter. Our first task, however, will be to trace the origins of *L'Immoraliste* and *La Porte étroite* in the early life and work of André Gide.

CHAPTER ONE

Origins

Gide's early work is indissolubly bound up with his real life experience, so that one is but the reflection of the other, and his writings take on the intensity of *drames vécus*. The conflicts they express are his own inner antagonisms: "J'ai passé toute ma jeunesse à opposer en moi deux parties de moi, qui peut-être ne demandaient pas mieux que de s'entendre. Par amour du combat, j'imaginais des luttes et je divisais ma nature."[1] The essential conflict was between the opposing claims of the spirit and of the flesh, between a deeply ingrained tendency towards mysticism and constraint and a no less ardent, though inhibited, longing for the satisfaction of the senses. André Walter became the embodiment, in literature, of these conflicting tendencies in the mind of André Gide, but with the greater emphasis placed on matters spiritual and the curbing of sensual desires. The year 1893, however, saw a violent reaction. Already there was evidence, in Gide's *Journal*, of an impatient chafing against the restraints of a puritanical *morale*: "O mon Dieu, qu'éclate cette morale trop étroite et que je vive, ah! pleinement; et donnez-moi la force de le faire, ah! sans crainte, et sans voir toujours que je m'en vais pécher."[2] The celebrated journey to Africa, that same year, consummated this liberation, so that, upon his return, Gide was able to write: "Je ne veux plus comprendre une morale qui ne permette et

[1] *Journal* (1893), p. 42 (Pléiade edition). [2] *Ibid.*, p. 34.

n'enseigne pas le plus grand, le plus beau, le plus libre emploi et développement de nos forces."[1]

This newly-won freedom found its literary expression in the exalted,
though artificial, lyricism of *Les Nourritures terrestres*, into which the
young Gide poured all the passionate ardour which he had displayed,
for a different purpose, in *Les Cahiers d'André Walter*. These two works
remain the *œuvres maîtresses*, the twin contrasting beacons which illuminate the whole of Gide's early work. Most of the other writings of
Gide's youth and early maturity, including *L'Immoraliste* and *La Porte
étroite*, are necessarily to be considered in relation to either, or both, of
these works, for they represent the two main phases in his intellectual
development as a young man. Henri Ghéon, in a lucid article written
as early as 1910, was right in seeing this as the basic evolution of the
author's youth—one which was completed with the publication of *Les
Nourritures terrestres* in 1897. Beyond this point, chronology matters
less than the impetus given to Gide's literary production by the fact
that he had already undergone this evolution and written these two
actes de foi. Subsequent works are developments, modifications or denials
of the basic attitudes inherent in these two major works. In successive
reactions, the pendulum swings now one way, now the other. Much
of *La Porte étroite* was already there in embryo in *André Walter*, just as
much of *L'Immoraliste* is already implicit in *Les Nourritures terrestres*,
and, from the point of view of Gide's evolution, it matters little that
one *récit* was composed before the other. One can say, of *La Porte étroite*
and *André Walter*, what Gide himself said of *L'Immoraliste* and *Les
Nourritures terrestres*, that the later book was "né entre les lignes du
premier."[2]

A curious phenomenon is here to be observed. So sensitive is the
balance of Gide's mind, so intense is his horror of being confined within
a single doctrine, that to portray one attitude is certain to evoke an
ardent nostalgia for its opposite, or, more significantly, for our understanding of *L'Immoraliste* and *La Porte étroite*, to provoke a subsequent
attempt to destroy, by criticism, any excess it may contain. "Je ne
faisais jamais que *ceci* ou que *cela*. Si je faisais ceci, cela m'en devenait
aussitôt regrettable."[3] For this pluralist, this *esprit sans pente*, any positive

[1] *Ibid.*, (1894), p. 52.
[2] Letter to Francis Jammes, 7 July 1902.
[3] Ménalque in *Les Nourritures terrestres, Romans*, (Pléiade edition) p. 183.

affirmation seemed always to be followed by the regret of having spoken, or by the fear that the thought expressed might not have been sufficiently *nuancé*. Hence the mystical ideal of virtue and self-sacrifice, as expressed in *André Walter*, could not be dissociated, in Gide's mind, from the excess to which such an attitude could lead, and the idea of *La Porte étroite* was born. Herein, too, lay the origin of that extraordinary trio of works which followed the *Nourritures terrestres—Saül, Le Roi Candaule* and *L'Immoraliste*, all three written as a necessary corrective to the doctrine of liberation and *disponibilité* preached by the master of Nathanaël, all three designed to reveal the dangers connected with such a doctrine. It was almost as though the author, having committed the unforgivable sin of adopting a specific attitude, could only expiate this sin by portraying a series of fictional heroes who would all be victims of an excessive attachment to this attitude.

Setting aside the author's ironic intentions in *L'Immoraliste* and *La Porte étroite*, these two *récits* present many similarities and points of contact with the two parent works. The general tone and atmosphere in each are visibly the same. Michel, falling seriously ill and then discovering for the first time the sensual enjoyment of life, aspires gradually to a doctrine which is basically the same as that of the narrator of *Les Nourritures terrestres*. Ménalque, who had appeared in the earlier book, reappears in *L'Immoraliste* as the embodiment of this doctrine and as an example for Michel to follow. The principles which he inculcates in Michel are those which re-echo triumphantly through the pages of *Les Nourritures*: the supreme value and uniqueness of the individual ("Ne t'attache en toi qu'à ce que tu sens qui n'est nulle part ailleurs qu'en toi-même" (p. 248); the necessity for *disponibilité, dépassement* and "dispossession" ("mon âme était l'auberge ouverte au carrefour; ce qui voulait entrer, entrait" (p. 185); the primacy of the instincts, of the senses and of feeling, and the importance of the present moment, essentially unique and irreplaceable ("Saisis de chaque instant la nouveauté irressemblable" (p. 167).

The very different atmosphere of *Les Cahiers d'André Walter* is re-echoed exactly in the much later *Porte étroite*. Even the basic subject is the same—the renunciation of earthly love in favour of a mystical communion of souls in an after-life. Alissa becomes the spiritual sister of André Walter in preferring God to human love, self-sacrifice to self-abandonment, and the path of virtue to a too easily attainable happiness. Certain passages occurring in *André Walter* and expressing the hero's similar preoccupation with a mystical ideal of virtue, which leads him to renounce Emmanuèle, would seem easily transposable from one book to the other: "Tu me connaissais bien si tu pensais que l'excès même de cette vertu m'exciterait à la suivre. Tu savais que les routes ardues et téméraires m'attirent . . . et qu'il faut un peu de folie pour rassasier mon orgueil." (p. 16). "Pas de vertu sans effort. Il faudrait l'effort sans l'espoir de la récompense." (p. 92). "La splendeur de la vertu, que d'abord je cherchais pour toi, m'éblouit peu à peu et m'attire elle-même." (p. 91). The identity of mood extends even to an identity of language, as when André Walter, pursuing his heroic ideal of self-effacement, remarks: "Te mériter plus en m'éloignant de toi." (p. 94)—a phrase which finds its echo in Jérôme's early attempt to deny himself the company of Alissa: "pensant la mieux mériter en m'éloignant d'elle aussitôt."[1]

In this way, *L'Immoraliste* and *La Porte étroite* present a close continuity with the major works of Gide's early youth. This continuity is a reality, because it is firmly rooted in the very life of André Gide. More than any other of his early fictional works, these two *récits* have their source in the author's true life experience. People, places and events in Gide's childhood and youth are here fed, with the inevitable modifications, into the fictional world he is creating. Critics have sufficiently stressed the autobiographical elements in both stories: the close links between Michel's awakening to life in Africa and Gide's spiritual re-birth in 1893 in a similar setting, the *souvenirs d'enfance* evoked nostalgically in *La Porte étroite*, the profound resemblance between the family properties of La Roque and Cuverville and their fictional counterparts, La Morinière and Fongueusemare. There is no need to dwell on these resemblances—it is enough to read Gide's reminiscences of his early life in *Si le Grain ne meurt*, for us to be convinced of their reality.

It should, however, be pointed out that the atmosphere of *La Porte étroite* evokes vividly the stifling, puritanical atmosphere of constraint which enveloped Gide's own childhood. Brought up in a typical French Protestant family, in which a strong sense of virtue and moral duty took precedence over worldly pleasures, Gide lived a childhood of uncompromising austerity, dominated by the influence of a severely religious, and possessive, mother. The Bible was for him, not just the Holy Book, but a living reality which was forever by his side and which

[1] *La Porte étroite*, p. 28.

proved to him a constant source of inspiration. Jérôme's natural inclina-
tions were, indeed, Gide's own: "Cet enseignement austère (de la
"porte étroite") trouvait une âme préparée, naturellement disposée au
devoir, et que l'exemple de mon père et de ma mère, joint à la discipline
puritaine à laquelle ils avaient soumis les premiers élans de mon coeur,
achevait d'incliner vers ce que j'entendais appeler: la vertu. Il m'était
aussi naturel de me contraindre qu'à d'autres de s'abandonner, et cette
rigueur à laquelle on m'asservissait, loin de me rebuter, me flattait."[1]
And the Bible is, for both Jérôme and Alissa, a living presence which
dominates the whole book, just as it dominated the childhood and early
youth of André Gide.

At the same time, the constraints of a Huguenot education posed
inevitable problems for a man who was dedicated to becoming an artist,
and it was only by reacting against these constraints, that Gide could
realise to the full his potentialities as a writer. It is this reaction which is
described in L'Immoraliste. As a child, Michel, like the real Gide, had
undergone "le grave enseignement huguenot de (sa) mère", absorbed its
principles and thereby acquired the taste for an austere way of life.[2] The
book relates how Michel makes the effort to escape from these shackles
and to discover his true self. But, in spite of the fact that he has deliberately rejected religion to become entirely dependent on himself, his
early religious training comes to the fore in certain almost involuntary
references to the Bible, as in the moving scene where Michel, on the
night before leaving Biskra, has a prophetic vision of the tragic destiny
which is to befall him.[3] As Michel admitted at the beginning of the
book, "je ne soupçonnais pas encore combien cette première morale
d'enfant nous maîtrise, ni quels plis elle laisse à l'esprit"[2]—a statement
which fits exactly the case of André Gide himself!

There is one relationship in Gide's life which calls for special comment,
being of great importance in the development both of L'Immoraliste and
La Porte étroite. This was, of course, his love for his cousin Madeleine,
which has been transposed into fictional form as Michel's love for
Marceline and Jérôme's love for Alissa. This relationship completely
dominated Gide's life and was at the origin of a great deal of his early
work. In Et nunc manet in te, Gide freely admits the profound influence

---

[1] La Porte étroite, p. 29.   [2] L'Immoraliste, p. 15.

[3] Ibid., pp. 55-6. This scene, and its biblical reference, are recalled ibid.
p. 178.

which Madeleine exerted on his intellectual development: "Il me semble que ce n'est qu'éveillé par mon amour pour elle que je pris conscience d'être et commençai vraiment d'exister. C'était à croire que rien de bon n'était en moi, qui ne me vînt d'elle".[1] And, if we are to believe him, all his work, up to Les Faux-Monnayeurs, was written with the express purpose of convincing and persuading Madeleine: "Tout cela n'est qu'un long plaidoyer."[2]

From this point of view, also, L'Immoraliste and La Porte étroite have their roots in Gide's early life. Taken together, they may be considered to present a dramatic and highly-coloured image of his relationship with Madeleine in the last decade of the 19th century. First, Madeleine's constant refusal between 1891 and 1894 to become engaged to her cousin[3] is reflected in Alissa's equally stubborn refusal to marry Jérôme, so that La Porte étroite becomes partly the drama of Gide's fiançailles. Then, as a consequence of his marriage in 1895, we witness the emergence of fresh problems, in particular how to reconcile the need for personal liberty and independence, so essential to Gide's nature, with the inevitable restrictions and compromises of married life. This dilemma, a source of ever-increasing conflict after 1895, is reflected in Michel's struggle for emancipation from conventional married happiness with the woman whom he never ceases to love. Thus L'Immoraliste becomes, in a sense, the drama of Gide's marriage and nostalgia for independence.

The chief characters, also, have a firm basis in Gide's own nature. To establish the links between Jérôme and his creator, what more revealing than Gide's description of his own youthful aspirations: "Mon amour enfantin (for Madeleine) se confondait avec mes premières ferveurs religieuses; ou du moins il entrait dans celles-ci, à cause d'elle, une sorte d'émulation. Il me semblait également, en m'approchant de Dieu, m'approcher d'elle et j'aimais, dans cette lente ascension, sentir le sol, autour d'elle et de moi, se rétrécir."[4] But, much more than Jérôme, Alissa, with her mystical piety, her taste for abnegation and sacrifice, represents an essential part of the young Gide, just as Michel, fervently seeking independence and self-understanding, represents the opposite, but no less powerful, tendencies in his nature. It is because Gide has

[1] Et nunc manet in te, in Journal et Souvenirs (Pléiade edn.), p. 1126.

[2] Ibid., p. 1157.

[3] cf. J. Schlumberger, Madeleine et André Gide.

[4] Et nunc manet in te, p. 1126.

extracted Alissa and Michel from the depths of his inner self, because they are in fact a part of his own flesh and blood—that their quest for an impossible ideal, in spite of the author's ironic intentions, still retains its essential nobility.

Neither events nor characters are, however, an exact reproduction of real life. These *récits* are not auto-biography, but fiction, and Gide has, quite legitimately, made the necessary modifications and transpositions which suit his artistic purposes. For him, as for all great writers, artistic truth presents a superior reality to that of real life. His chief characters are an integral part of himself, but at the same time considerably more. They represent, so to speak, possibilities, extensions or adaptations of his basic character. As with most great novelists, the mind of Gide swarms with a host of latent tendencies, many of them in conflict. The greater the novelist, the richer will be this multiplicity of hidden possibilities. Albert Thibaudet, in his analyses of Barrès, Flaubert and Stendhal, has shown how the novelist extracts from himself these inner possibilities and gives them life in his fictional heroes. The result is often a liberation of the author's secret frustrations or desires, embodied in characters like Emma Bovary or Julien Sorel. In Thibaudet's words, "le romancier authentique crée ses personnages avec les directions infinies de sa vie possible"[1] —a remark which Gide found so true that he was tempted to place it as an epigraph at the head of his *Faux-Monnayeurs*.

In the case of André Gide, opposing tendencies in his mind remain in conflict until liberated by the creation of the work of art. The latter thus offers a temporary resolution of the inner conflict and a sort of mental balance or harmony is achieved as a result. Gide, who was well aware of this phenomenon occurring within himself, likened it to Aristotle's purging of the passions. The process has been well described by him. Should one particular tendency in the author's mind become a troublesome obsession, the remedy is simple: isolate this tendency, attribute it to the character of a work of fiction, and watch it grow to alarming proportions. The therapeutic effect on the author is instantaneous: "on s'en défait du même coup."[2] It was, Gide said, almost as though his own thought held terrors for him: "de là vint ce besoin que j'eus de la prêter aux héros de mes livres pour la mieux écarter de moi."[3]

[1] *Réflexions sur le roman*, NRF, August 1912, p. 212.
[2] Letter to Scheffer (1902).
[3] Letter to Ch. Du Bos (1920), quoted by Lafille p. 471.

Such characters are not only "possibilities", but also "exaggerations" and "limitations" of the real Gide. In spite of his inner conflict, Gide is able to achieve, at the price of some considerable effort, a precarious balance between the opposing forces at war in his mind, whereas the fictional hero, obsessed by one dominant trait, cultivates this trait to the exclusion of all else. He thus achieves a singleness of purpose which goes far beyond the authentic Gide: "Ce qui manque à chacun de mes héros, que j'ai taillés dans ma chair même, c'est ce peu de bon sens qui me retient de pousser aussi loin qu'eux leurs folies."[1] Their exaggeration is, in many ways, a *limitation* of Gide, as the author himself indicated: "Si je n'étais que le héros . . . de l'*Immoraliste*, . . . c'est pour le coup que je me sentirais rétrécir."[2] And Professor Hytier very aptly points out the fact that the chief characters of Gide's *récits* are, indeed, all victims, victims of their excess, which has caused them to adopt a single attitude, instead of the widely-ranging diversity of attitudes characteristic of Gide himself. They are a limitation of Gide, because they do not possess his flexibility of thought, his ever-alert *disponibilité*.

In creating Michel and Ménalque Gide has carried his own individualist tendencies to a limit at which they become a danger for himself and for others. In this way, Gide succeeded momentarily in purging himself of his nostalgia for independence and his ardent desire for full self-realisation. Their excess enables him to achieve, in his own mind, a kind of temporary balance. It would be a mistake to identify them completely with Gide, for they are but latent "possibilities" of his nature: "ce n'est pas lui qu'il peint, mais ce qu'il peint, il aurait pu le devenir s'il n'était pas devenu tout lui-même."[3] Far from offering Ménalque as an ideal to be imitated, it is probable that Gide has endeavoured to show in this character his own principles carried to the excess which is inherent in every doctrine. He, as well as Michel, is a limitation of the true Gide: "c'est une création parasite qui prend sa vie à même la mienne et m'aura affaibli d'autant."[4]

Jérôme and Alissa are, for their part, the embodiment of Gide's own spiritual and religious aspirations, but, again, with the unfavourable judgment implied by excess. Jérôme is full of Gide's own mystical fervour and keen sensibility as a youth, but separates from his creator in

[1] *Journal des Faux-Monnayeurs*, p. 94.
[2] *Journal*, Sept. 1909, p. 276.   [3] *Journal* (1927) (Pléiade edition) p. 829.
[4] Letter to Marcel Drouin, 24 Jan. 1896.

his extreme passivity and "flabbiness". The natural shyness, uncertainty and nervousness of the young Gide are carried, in Jérôme, to such an exaggerated extreme that the character appears almost incapable of any decisive action. But the negative role of Jérôme was also rendered inevitable by Gide's conception of the story, in which he wished the full light to be projected on the evolution of Alissa. It is, indeed, Alissa who is the real protagonist of *La Porte étroite*, in spite of Jérôme's importance as narrator. Alissa herself is a composite figure. She is at once Madeleine and André Gide, but at the same time can be identified with neither. Recalling Madeleine by her purity, austerity and piety, she becomes, in addition, the victim of an excessively rigid devotion to an ideal, whereas, in the case of Madeleine, "il n'y eut jamais rien de forcé ni d'excessif dans sa vertu".[1] Similarly, while embodying Gide's own religious tendencies, Alissa carries them to an almost impossible limit, to a hypothetical extreme which the real Gide would never have countenanced. By creating this character, the author was able to provide an outlet for the disturbing religious conflict which so often divided his mind. The work of art serves, once again, as a form of liberation, a personal catharsis.

CHAPTER TWO

Techniques

"Le point de vue esthétique est le seul où il faille se placer pour parler de mon œuvre sainement."

(Gide, *Journal*, 25 April, 1918)

The Classical Artist

The supreme originality of Gide's early *récits* lies in their combination of intimate personal experience with a technique that strove to exclude entirely the presence of the author, "cette extraordinaire puissance de vie personnelle et d'objectivité sereine", as Jean Hytier put it.[2] Gide's view is essentially that of the classical artist, whose aim is to present

[1] *Et nunc manet in te*, p. 1148 (Pléiade edition).
[2] J. Hytier, *André Gide*, p. 175.

characters in action, who reveal themselves sufficiently by what they say or do, without any need for the author to intervene and explain motives or draw conclusions. Gide remained consistently true to himself on this point, ever since the publication of his first work, *André Walter*, in which the somewhat pale, anaemic hero defined his attitude to the novel as follows: "La vérité voudrait, je crois, qu'il n'y ait pas de conclusion: elle doit ressortir du récit même, sans qu'il soit besoin d'une péripétie qui la fasse flagrante. Jamais les choses ne se concluent: c'est l'homme qui tire les conclusions des choses."[1]

Gide would willingly subscribe to Thibaudet's view on the infinite suggestibility of a work of art, feeling that the richer it is, the more possibilities of interpretation it will evoke in the discerning reader. As he suggested in the *Journal d'Edouard (Faux-Monnayeurs)*, the average novelist does not make sufficient allowance for the imagination of the reader, and kills the book by artificially imposing on it a conclusion. Such an attitude accounts for the hermetic quality of much of Gide's very early work, which deliberately offers a tenacious resistance to any easy comprehension and consequently falls within the category of those books that Gide prefers, "les œuvres qu'on ne comprend pas bien d'abord, qui ne se livrent pas sans réticence et sans pudeur."[2] His chief aim is not to provide the reader with ready-made solutions to vital problems, but to invite him to think them out for himself.

Nowhere is Gide's objectivity more conspicuous than in *L'Immoraliste* and *La Porte étroite*, where the author deliberately refrains from passing any judgment on his chief characters and invites the reader's active collaboration in forming his own opinion from the events related. In the preface to *L'Immoraliste*, Gide categorically affirms his intentions: "je n'ai voulu faire en ce livre non plus acte d'accusation qu'apologie, et me suis gardé de juger. . . je n'ai cherché de rien prouver, mais de bien peindre et d'éclairer bien ma peinture."[3] What is true of *L'Immoraliste* appears to be even more true of *La Porte étroite*, but the appearance of greater objectivity created by this book is to some extent an illusion—an illusion brought about by the different technique of *La Porte étroite*. Here Jérôme's characteristically flat and mostly dispassionate narration of the events alternates with the reproduction of Alissa's letters and diary, which are largely quoted by Jérôme without comment, rather in

[1] *André Walter*, 1952 edition, p. 94. [2] *Nouveaux Prétextes*, p. 169.
[3] *L'Immoraliste*, pp. 1-3.

the manner of a lawyer bringing forward documents as evidence. The truth is, however, that both books are equally fine examples of impartiality and detachment on the part of the author.

An even more revealing light is thrown on this fundamental feature of Gide's art by comparing the final text of *L'Immoraliste* with the first manuscript of the novel, which is now preserved in the *Fonds Gide* at the *Bibliothèque Doucet*, Paris. A certain number of deletions from this first version bear eloquent testimony to Gide's desire to preserve the artistic purity of the *récit* by letting events and action speak for themselves rather than have them interpreted for us by the narrator. Some of the essential themes of the novel are involved in these deletions, but Gide has preferred to give the reader full credit for his intelligence and allow him the pleasure of discovering them for himself by a perceptive reading of the text.

What is the basic theme of *L'Immoraliste* but that the quest for one's unique individuality is incompatible, or at least in sharp conflict with marital happiness? In the first manuscript, this theme was stated unequivocally by Ménalque in the course of his final conversation with Michel. When the narrator indicates his envy for Ménalque's untrammelled way of life, the latter sees this as completely unjustified, as illogical as if *he* were to envy Michel's more static happiness: "Serai-je assez fou pour ne pas me rendre compte que le bonheur d'un foyer, d'une famille est incompatible avec la forme de vie que je mène? Soyez donc assez sage pour comprendre que la nature de mes joies est incompatible avec la vie que vous vous êtes taillée." Ménalque's main role in *L'Immoraliste* is to serve as a mouthpiece for certain philosophical ideas, and Gide must presumably have felt it excessive that this character should, in addition, spell out in so many words one of the book's main themes. To pronounce such a judgment is surely the prerogative of the reader, after a balanced consideration of the events of the story. In any case, the author subsequently deleted this passage and expressed the idea in briefer and more general terms: "Envier le bonheur d'autrui, c'est folie; on ne saurait pas s'en servir."[1]

To anyone who reads *L'Immoraliste* with due care, it must be apparent that the remarkable power of sympathy that the author bestows on Michel, is at least partly responsible for his downfall. This becomes increasingly evident in the second half of the story, and, to this extent,

[1] *L'Immoraliste*, p. 122.

the book becomes a satire of the dangers of excessive *disponibilité*, that Gidean quality *par excellence*. In the final text, Gide carefully establishes Michel's capacity for active sympathy with the workers on his property (pp. 133-4), so that he feels acutely their fatigue, their thirst and their pain. Earlier versions, notably the first *brouillon* already mentioned, and also a second manuscript, referred to in the Pléiade edition of Gide's *Romans*, had developed even further this propensity of Michel: as he observed them, he had himself experienced the numbness in the hands of washerwomen, the aching backs and shoulders of woodcutters or of the men who hauled the barges along the river banks. But it is, significantly, only in the first *brouillon* that occurs the following sentence, later erased by Gide for reasons which are obvious: it offered too explicit a statement of a tendency which should only have become clear in the light of subsequent events in the story: "Et si j'insiste tant ici c'est que rien peut-être ne contribua davantage à l'éparpillement et à la désagréga-tion de mon être." To tell the reader this, in advance, Gide would feel, is to suppress three quarters of his enjoyment, to deprive him of the pleasure of 'deviner peu à peu', as Mallarmé put it.

Finally, it should be clear to the discerning reader by the end of the book that Michel, in striving to achieve greater self-understanding and sincerity, was merely pursuing an illusion, and that his quest was a wretched failure. But to prejudge the issue by making such a statement in the actual text of the novel, was an unforgivable sin in the eyes of a supremely detached artist like Gide. Hence the author's deletion of the following passage from the first manuscript, which acknowledged both the failure of Michel's quest and his *consciousness* of his failure: "Décidé-ment je me pipais moi-même en prétendant chercher une plus ou moins grande sincérité! Certes tous les anciens instincts restent dans l'homme. Je réveillais tout ce que je croyais découvrir." Was it not better, in the interests of objectivity, that the reader should arrive at his own personal judgment of Michel, based on the narration of the events? "Malheur aux livres qui concluent!" (Gide).

The suppression of the last two passages considered can be said to serve a two-fold purpose: firstly, to keep the artist entirely detached from his work and prevent him from passing judgment on his characters, in accordance with his expressed view that "les idées ne devraient être exprimées que par l'action."[1] At the same time, however, it served to

[1] *Lettres à Angèle*, O.C. III, 166.

keep the narrator, Michel, deluded about himself and his motives. Part of Michel's tragedy will be his unconscious self-deception about the nobility of his mission, and in order to draw the fullest value from this tragic ambiguity, it was vital that Gide should preserve his narrator's delusions of grandeur. Such a person would hardly admit to "la désagrégation de (son) être" nor to the utter futility of his quest for sincerity!

The principal tendency of Gide's *récits*, then, is towards the virtual withdrawal of the author's presence from the fictional world he has created, which becomes a world existing in its own right. This is not to say that the writer has not lived and suffered intensely with his characters, a fact already apparent from the manner in which we have seen Gide draw on his own life-experience to create them. Indeed, one could say that they are doubly a part of him—firstly, in their original inspiration, which has its sources in the author's life, and, secondly, in their subsequent elaboration in the mind of the novelist, as he strives to give them an independent existence of their own. For, during the process of artistic creation, the characters again become an intimate part of their creator's being, to the extent to which the author literally takes upon himself, by sympathy, the qualities of his heroes. Few writers have possessed so active a power of sympathy with other people, as did Gide—a power which, in turn, he confers on many of his fictional heroes, including Michel, Alissa, Marceline and even Jérôme! Here is the very source of his *disponibilité*, of that unlimited capacity for embracing the most widely divergent points of view, which led Claudel to describe him as *un esprit sans pente*. Because his mind became so absorbed by the thoughts and emotions of others, because his heart beat only in sympathy with others (to use his own expression), discussion became difficult for him, for he immediately tended to abandon his own point of view.[1]

Gide rightly saw in this power of sympathy the key to his whole character and to his literary work. It is important to realise, for a clear understanding of his processes of literary creation, Gide's capacity for escaping from himself and assuming an alien form. The author has, indeed, given a very vivid description of this power of absorption in another being: "Rien n'est fait si, ce personnage que j'assume, je n'ai pas su vraiment le devenir, jusqu'à me donner le change... C'est revenir à moi qui m'embarrasse, car, en vérité, je ne sais plus bien qui je suis; ou, si

---

[1] cf. *Journal des Faux-Monnayeurs*, p. 87.

l'on préfère: je ne suis jamais, je deviens."[1] It is because he was able to *become* Michel (and not only because he was re-living true life experiences) that certain pages of *L'Immoraliste*—notably those in which the hero falls ill with tuberculosis and then, during convalescence, experiences a profound sensual re-awakening—vibrate with the intensity of real life. It was because he was able to *become* Alissa (and not only because his story was based on a poignant chapter of his own life) that the *Journal d'Alissa* awakened echoes of a tragic and personally felt inner *angoisse*. It was, above all, because he was able to *become* Jérôme that he was able to create so convincingly a character who was in some respects almost the antithesis of the author himself. In the face of such complexity, what becomes of the terms *subjective* and *objective*? In Gide's own words, "ces mots perdent ici tout leur sens"[2] and, in speaking of the author's objectivity, we should at once hasten to refer to the warm human sympathy which tempers, and illuminates, the detachment of the literary artist.

The creations of the greatest French writers have been illumined by a similar combination of detachment and sympathy. Would the impact of Emma Bovary have been so great without Flaubert's deeply felt nostalgia for her Romantic dreams, which makes her an unforgettable human being, in spite of the equally mordant irony with which he devastates her? This is the very basis of Gide's classicism, which lies also in the restraint and balance of his literary work, in the importance which he always attached to artistic values and style. Like the great classical writers of the 17th century, his profound interest was in the analysis of human feelings, which though particular in their origin, become universal in their application. The art which is revealed in *L'Immoraliste* and *La Porte étroite* clearly separates them from the products of the literary schools of Gide's youth. Although his earliest work was impregnated with the complacent narcissism of the Symbolist poets, towards the end of the 19th century a strong reaction is visible in his attitude, which is marked by a return to greater realism and a turning towards contemporary subjects, instead of the biblical and mythological themes which characterise his early treatises and fiction. The first rewarding fruits of this reaction are to be found, not in the *Nourritures terrestres*, still too artificial and stilted in its excess of lyricism, but in *Paludes*, and especially *L'Immoraliste*. That this return to realism was not achieved

[1] *Journal* (1927) pp. 829-30.   [2] *Journal* (1922) p. 737.

without considerable effort on Gide's part, is attested by a letter[1] dated January 1918 and accompanying the first manuscript of *L'Immoraliste*: "J'eus le plus grand mal à reprendre pied dans le réel et à résigner les théories de l'école (je veux dire celle que formaient les disciples de Mallarmé)—qui tendaient à présenter la réalité comme une contingence accidentelle et à en vouloir échapper l'œuvre d'art."

The realism to which Gide aspired was, however, far removed from the realism of the *Ecole Naturaliste*, which in its preoccupation with the minutiae and trivialities of description, aimed more at a slavish imitation, a photographic reproduction, of the external world. Gide's reality is a heightened reality, one which is transformed by the magic power of art, and he has nothing but scorn for the interminable descriptions of the *romanciers naturalistes*. The *Journal d'Edouard*, in the *Faux-Monnayeurs*, exactly puts Gide's own point of view: "La précision ne doit pas être obtenue par le détail du récit, mais bien, dans l'imagination du lecteur, par deux ou trois traits, exactement à la bonne place."[2] It is precisely this classical ideal which Gide seeks to achieve in *L'Immoraliste* and *La Porte étroite*. A few sober strokes are all that is needed to evoke Michel's house in the desert (pp. 9-10), Marceline's physical appearance (p. 18) and Ménalque's *visage de pirate* (pp. 115-16). The first description of Alissa (pp. 19-20) has a quite vague, even idealised, quality—we learn practically nothing about her physical features, except for the sadness of her smile and the extraordinarily high elevation of her eyebrows! Even when her external appearance assumes a considerable importance in the unfolding of the plot, as at the moment of the *dépoétisation affreuse* to which she submits herself—even there, Gide permits himself only a summary five lines of description (p. 147). The first manuscript of *L'Immoraliste* contains, significantly, many passages which the born classicist in Gide later rejected as superfluous, as adding nothing to the dramatic impact of the story—descriptions of native towns and villages, of walks in the neighbourhood of Biskra with Marceline, and, above all, long descriptions of native children encountered in the course of Michel's sojourn in Africa.

At the same time, when it is a question of achieving a dramatic effect, establishing an atmosphere or developing a character, Gide is not averse to using descriptions for this purpose. Here again, we are inevitably

---

[1] In the Bibliothèque Doucet, Paris.
[2] *Les Faux-Monnayeurs*, (Pléiade edition) p. 1000.

reminded of a great work of art like *Madame Bovary*, where, in spite of the criticism which has been levelled at their excessive length, it could be shown that there is hardly one of Flaubert's descriptions which is not dramatically relevant to the work as a whole. Thus, in *L'Immoraliste*, as Michel, recovering from his serious illness in the desert of North Africa, gradually becomes aware of the surroundings which are to play a decisive part in his physical re-awakening, Gide gives a full description of this environment (pp. 27-8). Similarly, in *La Porte étroite*, the house and garden of Fongueusemare, which are to provide the essential atmosphere for the whole story, and even to play their part in the symbolism of the novel, are described in full from the very outset (pp. 8-10). Finally, if the other characters of *La Porte étroite* are sketched in the very briefest of outlines—when it is a question of Lucile Bucolin, who makes only a fleeting appearance in the story, yet possesses an important symbolic value as the embodiment of the sensual desires which torment Alissa, then a fuller portrait is called for, and we have the vivid descriptions of pp. 14-16.

*   *   *

The First-Person Narrator

The most striking way in which Gide achieves objectivity in his *récits* is by his use of the first-person narrator device. At first glance, it may seem something of a paradox that the use of the first person should achieve such an aim, but it will be seen that it is a borrowed first-person, and not Gide speaking in his own name. In fact, Gide well summed up the point himself in an expressive formula: "Ce 'JE' est pour moi le comble de l'objectivité."[1] It is not difficult to see why this should be so. No comments or explanations are provided by the author, who, as far as the reader is concerned, simply does not exist. He stands aside and effaces himself completely behind his narrator, who is also the hero, or one of the chief characters, of the *récit*. This character at once takes on an apparent authenticity, a third-dimensional quality which gives the story greater realism. At the same time, an illusion of greater intimacy is achieved, as a result of the direct *rapprochement* which is established between the narrator and the reader.

Here, then, is an extremely economical, and subtle, device for

[1] Letter to Christian Beck (16 October 1909).

portraying the character of a fictional hero, and one which always proved tempting to Gide:[1] to let the hero reveal his character *directly* by his narration of events which have had a decisive influence on the course of his life. Thus Michel's forthright, callous nature is revealed by his account of the tragic events of his marriage. The passive, spineless and highly suggestible character of Jérôme emerges clearly from his narration of the events that lead to Alissa's self-sacrifice and death. In *La Porte étroite*, however, the technique is more complex, for we have here really two complementary *récits* and two narrators—Jérôme's version of the story, and Alissa's version of a part of it, as recorded in her Diary. Illuminating flashes of light pass from one version to the other to reveal, and to expose inconsistencies in, the characters both of Jérôme and Alissa.

Gide did not immediately hit upon such a technique. The writing of *La Porte étroite* gave him at the outset a considerable amount of trouble, and unpublished *brouillons* in the Bibliothèque Doucet reveal his first unsuccessful attempts to write the story in the third person. Among these is a highly dramatic, even melodramatic, version of the crucial scene in Alissa's room, where Jérôme first becomes aware of his love for his cousin. Here the presence of the author was, alas! all too visible, and at variance with his desire for impartiality, expressed in a note in the margin of one of these fragments: "Il faut éviter de se poser plutôt au point de vue de l'un que de l'autre". There is evidence also of an intermediate stage, in which Jérôme, in a similar state of apathy and disillusionment to that of Michel, relates his story to a sympathetic acquaintance in the abandoned garden at Fongueuse-mare. But, for Gide, this was to adopt the point of view of only one of his two main characters, and he finally solved the dilemma by placing the versions of *both* Jérôme *and* Alissa side by side in the body of the work.

It is above all the inconsistencies in his characters, and their unconscious distortion of the events, that Gide is eager to reveal by his use of the first person narrator device. From the very beginning of his career, Gide was fascinated by what he called the "retro-action" of a subject upon itself: "Un homme en colère raconte une histoire; voilà le sujet d'un livre. Un homme racontant une histoire, ne suffit pas; il faut que ce soit un homme en colère, et qu'il y ait un constant rapport entre

[1] Cf. *Journal des Faux-Monnayeurs*, p. 34.

la colère de cet homme et l'histoire racontée."[1] The state of mind of the character will then, as Gide pointed out in the *Journal des Faux-Monnayeurs*, necessarily entail a slight distortion of the events he is relating, and this he invites the reader's active collaboration in discovering for himself: "une sorte d'intérêt vient, pour le lecteur, de ce seul fait qu'il ait à *rétablir*."[2] It is very important to note this fact for the two *récits* we are considering. The three narrators involved in the stories are all suffering from delusions about themselves, and these delusions inevitably affect, and even distort, each person's account of the events. It is for us to *rétablir*, with the aid of the scraps of evidence which Gide disperses throughout the *récits*.

We can, in addition, sense in the narratives of both Michel and Jérôme a subconscious desire for self-justification, a wish to prove to themselves, and to others, that they were right in acting as they did. Subtly, Gide has made it appear that one of their chief motives in undertaking the narration lies in this uncertainty about themselves, in this eagerness to *convince*. This is already apparent in the reaction of Michel's audience to his finished narrative: "Il nous semblait, hélas! qu'à nous la raconter, Michel avait rendu son action plus légitime."[3] And, when he says, in his state of complete apathy at the end of the book, "je dois me prouver à moi-même que je n'ai pas outrepassé mon droit,"[4] we feel that his entire *récit* has been partly an unconscious attempt to convince himself, and his audience, of that very fact. Similarly, in *La Porte étroite*, in spite of Jérôme's declared intention to undertake the narrative so as to relive, nostalgically, his past memories, we cannot help feeling that he also is seeking his self-justification, and the approval of the reader, by putting down the facts of the story. He asks us in effect: faced with this situation which I have described to you, how could I have acted otherwise than I did, or in any way be blamed for my actions? It is for this reason that both narrators emphasise the factual accuracy of their account. Because they seek to draw their own justification from the *récit*, they are careful to insist that they are simply setting down the events as they occurred, without any falsification or any attempt to deck them out in the garb of art: "je n'aurai recours à aucune invention pour les rapiécer ou les joindre";[5] "que m'importe à moi ce récit, s'il cesse d'être véritable?"[6]

---

[1] *Journal* (1893), p. 41.   [2] *Journal des Faux-Monnayeurs*, p. 34.
[3] *L'Immoraliste* p. 185.   [4] *L'Immoraliste*, p. 186.
[5] *La Porte étroite*, p. 7.   [6] *L'Immoraliste*, p. 181.

What, now, is the essential nature of this blindness, or self-delusion, that Gide imposes on each of his narrators? In each case, it resolves itself into that basic conflict which was so constant a preoccupation in Gide's work—between *l'être* and *le paraître*, between the real self and the mask, between true motives, which often lie hidden in the sub-conscious, and apparent ones, which we deceive ourselves into regarding as real, and which make unconscious hypocrites of us all. Here, indeed, was to be the fundamental theme of *Les Faux-Monnayeurs*, so aptly expressed in the deeply symbolic title of the novel. Michel's tragedy lies in the fact that, while pursuing in reality a selfishly hedonistic quest for pleasure and self-gratification, he deludes himself into believing that he is seeking a noble ideal of self-realisation. Similarly, Alissa deceives herself in believing that her quest for God is a completely disinterested and noble self-sacrifice for the sake of Jérôme, while in reality it is partly motivated by both feelings of false pride and a deeply-rooted fear of life. Egotism is at the basis of Michel's actions, just as much as it is an excess of pride which spurs on Alissa. As for Jérôme, his blindness lies in his failure to realise the heavy burden of responsibility *he* must share with Alissa for the tragic events which lead to her death.

One of Gide's chief preoccupations, in composing the two stories, was to keep his narrators at least partly deluded about their motives for action, so that, in the course of the narrative, they tend to incriminate themselves by what they either say or do. The attentive reader is thus invited to read between the lines and attempt to distinguish true motives from false. Michel is at least partly lucid about himself when the events of his story are over and he is able to look back on them with some detachment. For instance, he now realises that, during his last frenzied journey to Africa with an ailing Marceline, his actions were not always prompted by a disinterested consideration for his wife's health and happiness. This was his fond delusion at the time, but he recognises now his error. "Par quelle aberration, quel aveuglement obstiné, quelle volontaire folie, me persuadai-je, et surtout tâchai-je de lui persuader qu'il lui fallait plus de lumière encore et de chaleur?"[1] He is able at last to perceive the true motives for some of his actions at that time. In endeavouring to convince Marceline—and himself—that there was no point in prolonging their stay in Switzerland, because the full benefit of the mountain air had been secured, and that it only remained to

[1] *L'Immoraliste*, p. 170.

complete her cure in the warmer climate of Italy, Michel now realised that he had sub-consciously been seeking an escape from the boredom he himself felt in the Swiss mountains (p. 163). Similarly, he can now discern the real motives which lay behind his decision to order the best wines for their meals—ostensibly to stimulate Marceline's flagging appetite: "Je me persuadais qu'elle y prenait grand goût, tant m'amusaient ces crus étrangers que nous expérimentions chaque jour".[1]

In spite of this partial lucidity, there is always a deeper level at which Michel is still deceiving himself. He is apathetic, listless and disillusioned as the result of Marceline's death, but he is in no way convinced that his mission has been a failure—or at least, he refuses to admit its failure. Hence his determination to *recommencer à neuf*, and to continue the process of "dispossession" which he had left uncompleted (p. 186). Hence his constant re-assurances (for the benefit of his audience as well as for himself) that he is now a tower of strength, that he still feels moved only by the noblest of sentiments: "Qu'ai-je besoin de tout cela? Je suis devenu fort, à présent."[2] "Je ne sens rien que de noble en moi."[3] He invents specious arguments to justify the systematic self-dispossession which he undertakes in the last part of the book, and seeks even to convince himself, by a form of rationalisation, that he is doing it not only for his own sake, but for Marceline as well. He takes sumptuous apartments at St. Moritz and justifies the expense by referring to his wife's precarious state of health and her consequent need for comfort: "Marceline, elle, a besoin de luxe; elle est faible. Ah! pour elle je veux dépenser tant et tant que . . ."[4]

In spite of the obvious sincerity of his love for Marceline, it is evident here that Michel is merely deceiving himself and that his concern for his wife serves as a cloak for motives which are basically egotistical.

Equally pathetic is Michel's readiness to blame everything but himself for the state of apathy and dejection in which he appears before his friends. To blame himself would be to admit the failure of his whole enterprise and a convenient scapegoat must be found. Human failings are frequently attributed to causes which are beyond the power of man to control, like the weather, and Michel, conveniently and somewhat complacently, finds in the climate of the desert sufficient explanation for the destruction of his will-power: "Ce climat, je crois, en est cause.

---

[1] *Ibid*. p. 161.   [2] *Ibid*. p. 160.
[3] *Ibid*. p. 174.   [4] *L'Immoraliste* p. 161.

Rien ne décourage autant la pensée que cette persistance de l'azur. Ici toute recherche est impossible, tant la volupté suit de près le désir."[1]

Jérôme and Alissa are, no less than Michel, the victims of their own delusions and of that form of unconscious hypocrisy which is revealed by a character's use of rationalisation. Alissa, like Michel, is partially lucid about herself, and succeeds in locating within the hidden recesses of her mind some of the many temptations of egotism and false pride which are eventually to cause her downfall. She even makes a strenuous effort to resist these temptations, as when she abandons her diary for a time, because it had become "le complaisant miroir devant lequel (son) âme s'apprête." But she, like Michel, is constantly deceiving herself at a still deeper level. Striving to avoid pride, and seek humility, she falls into an even deeper abyss of pride. Dimly conscious of her real motives for action, which lie partly in the intoxication of self-sacrifice sought after as an ideal in itself, and partly in the desire to prove to herself that she was capable of it,[2] she nevertheless is impelled, subconsciously, to invent reasons for her action which will ease her conscience and preserve her self-esteem. Thus she deludes herself into thinking that she is nobly sacrificing herself so as to enable Jérôme to reach God (p. 186)—in its way, as specious a rationalisation as was Michel's belief in the disinterestedness of his own actions.

As far as Jérôme is concerned, it is obvious from his account of the events that he had at the time very little understanding about what was going on in Alissa's mind. Now that he has access to her diary, he realises, it is true, the extent to which her love for him continued until the very end, but a more clear-sighted person than Jérôme would not have failed to have detected this much earlier from certain undercurrents in the very letters which gave warning of her coming renunciation. The general tone of these letters is austere and uncompromising, but with hidden undertones of passion[3] which Alissa is unable to conceal and which would have encouraged a less passive suitor to press on with determination to the eventual and undoubted triumph of his love.

Again, faced with the *dépoétisation* of Alissa, Jérôme immediately arrives at the wrong explanation, and one which most flatters his own ego. The whole of his *récit* shows us to what extent it was Alissa who,

---

[1] *Ibid.* p. 186.
[2] "N'en étais-je donc point capable?" (*La Porte étroite*, p. 180).
[3] cf. pp. 130-1 and p. 142.

in their relationship, always called the tune, with the highly suggestible Jérôme following lamely behind—an impression confirmed by a reading of her diary, in which all the initiative for the vital decisions affecting their future clearly comes from Alissa alone. And yet Jérôme, that past master of inaction, claims that it was *his* influence on *her* which brought them to this tragic impasse: was it not he who had made an idol of Alissa, putting her on a lofty pedestal of virtue, so that, when left to herself, she had simply descended from the heights "où mon unique effort l'avait placée"[1] and reverted to her own mediocre level? So extravagant a supposition, belied by all the facts which are presented for the reader's judgment, serves to emphasise the pathetic delusions which affect Jérôme's understanding both of Alissa and of himself.

Irony

The technique of the deluded narrator, as Gide understood it, inevitably led to a widespread use of irony in the *récit*. Since the author had deliberately absented himself from the narrative, and since the narrator was himself labouring under delusions about his role in the story or as regards the effectiveness of his actions, the sole method of enlightening the reader was precisely by the use of such a device. And Gide, throughout both stories, has made a most subtle use of irony, of which the example just discussed will serve as a good illustration. There, as we have seen, Jérôme's delusion, towards the end of the story, was that it was his effort alone which had been responsible for elevating Alissa to such dizzy heights of virtue. A close reading of Alissa's diary, however, makes it clear that the greatest efforts to attain virtue were made by Alissa herself and that these efforts were often accompanied by the most heartbreaking inner conflict. On the contrary, it was *she* who had urged on *Jérôme* towards virtue, as we see from the diary, when she refers to her heart as being "un coeur désireux jusqu'à la folie de le pousser jusqu'à ce sommet de vertu que je désespérais d'atteindre."[2] The irony, in this instance, clearly arises from the juxtaposition, within the same text, of two completely contrasting interpretations—one nullifies, and cancels out, the other; the second destroys the first by its implications, and much more subtly

---

[1] *La Porte étroite*, p. 160.
[2] *La Porte étroite*, p. 200.

and effectively by bare statement than by lines of detailed analysis or explanation on the part of the author.

Before proceeding to a close examination of Gide's use of irony in the two *récits*, we should first clarify the general principles involved in its use. Both works are stories of an ambitious quest which ends in failure, and related by narrators who deceive themselves about their motives for action or their responsibility for this failure. Both Michel and Alissa, though disillusioned, still believe in the validity, and even the nobility, of their mission, and it is the role of irony to destroy these illusions for the discerning reader. By reading the story carefully, the latter is thus enabled to substitute true motives for false, and to come to his own conclusions about the success, or failure, of each quest. This is achieved by the ironic juxtaposition of contrasting motives (as seen in the example above), by conflict between stated intentions and the actual events which transpire, or by ironic parallels which are set up between two similar sets of happenings. Nowhere does the author intervene with any comments, and the narrator himself is not conscious of the irony, but the facts related speak eloquently for themselves.

In *L'Immoraliste*, there soon appears a considerable discrepancy between Michel's declared motives and intentions in the first and second parts and his accomplishment of these intentions in the final part—in other words, the events and experiences related by him at the end of the book distort, and make a mockery of, the purity of his original motives. Although Michel is hardly aware of it, all the episodes of his last frenzied journey to Africa with Marceline combine, ironically, to emphasise the futility, and failure, of his attempt to carry out the principles of Ménalque. The would-be superman cuts a very sorry figure indeed when placed alongside the ideal figure he sought to realise. Deluding himself that he is courageously pushing forward to a difficult ideal of self-realisation and self-understanding, he is in reality abandoning himself to a facile quest for pleasure and self-indulgence. It is only at the end of the narrative that we realise the full irony of the biblical quotation which Gide placed under the title of the book in the form of an epigraph: "Je te loue, ô mon Dieu, de ce que tu m'as fait créature si admirable".

Ménalque, in the course of his final conversation with Michel, had made clear his attitude to the past, and to the recollection of memories of the past: "Je ne veux pas me souvenir . . . C'est du parfait oubli d'hier

que je crée la nouvelleté de chaque heure . . . Je n'aime pas regarder en
arrière, et j'abandonne au loin mon passé."[1] In "dispossessing" himself,
Michel had sought to put this principle into practice, but the events
of his last journey to Africa prove him to be still the victim of *le souvenir*.
What was his whole journey but a nostalgic pursuit of the memories
that had meant so much to him at the time of his convalescence—of
people, places and objects that vividly evoked for him the period of
his re-awakening to life (pp. 175-6)? And now that Marceline is dead,
he cannot help recalling with regret the happy moments of that last
fatal journey, like the sleigh-rides in the snow at St-Moritz (pp. 163-4).
"Le passé détesté reprend sa force", and resists all Michel's efforts to
vanquish it.

The greatest single obstacle in the way of Michel's full self-realisation is the reality of his love for Marceline. It is this which turns the
apparent strength of a Nietzschean-type superman into the frailty
and weakness of an ordinary mortal like ourselves. Here again, the
events make a mockery of Michel's original intentions and emphasise,
by irony, the utter failure of his mission. If, in the course of the final
journey to Africa, he abandons his ailing wife for an hour to go in
search of new experiences and new sensations, he is unable to do so
without the most agonising qualms of conscience, which urge him to
return at once to her bedside. Instead of plunging relentlessly onward in
his quest for greater self-knowledge, this 'raté de l'individualisme'
hesitates, stricken with remorse, tries desperately to whip up his flagging
will-power, then, like a small child, asserting himself out of spite,
deliberately prolongs his absence. Is this the action of a true disciple of
Ménalque? Michel implicitly admits his failure by his own account of
the events:—"parfois j'appelais à moi ma volonté, protestais contre cette
emprise, me disais: n'est-ce que cela que tu vaux, faux grand'homme!—
et me contraignais à faire durer mon absence;—mais je rentrais alors
les bras chargés de fleurs."[2]

The greatest indication of Michel's defeat, however, comes from the
general air of disillusionment, sadness and bitterness which surrounds
the events related in the last part of the story. Where are the thrill
and the excitement of self-discovery, or the happiness which should
emerge from the successful realisation of the true self, we may ask
ourselves? Michel's account of the events is a veritable self-indictment.

[1] *L'Immoraliste*, p. 123-4.   [2] *L'Immoraliste*, p. 167.

Hardly an exclamation of joy or true pleasure, but one long cry of frustration and heartbreak: "Quelle déconvenue!" (p. 176); "Il y a là comme une banqueroute . . ." (*ibid*); "mon intolérable tristesse" (*ibid.*); "Ce n'est plus, comme avant, une souriante harmonie" (p. 178); "mornes étapes sur la route plus morne encore, interminable" (*ibid.*); "O goût de cendres! O lassitude! Tristesse du surhumain effort." (p. 180). Once more, the narrator's noble intentions are negated, and destroyed, by the terrible irony of the actual events.

In *L'Immoraliste*, irony is also generated by the very symmetry of the novel's construction, which we shall be considering in a later section. The journey of the first part is almost exactly paralleled by the journey at the end, and events in the first journey find their ironic counterpart in the events of the second. Distant, mocking echoes are set up, which, reverberating in the mind of the reader, reinforce the sense of bitter failure aroused in him by Michel's quest. Thus the fight with a coach-man (p. 72), which establishes Michel's virility and leads to a brief period of marital happiness, is paralleled, and mocked, by the episode of the coachman in the last part of the story (p. 170), where a very different reaction is provoked! In this final section, the same people and the same places recur systematically, but as though seen through a distorting mirror. We return to Syracuse, yet our nostrils are no longer assailed there by the perfume of the lemon trees in the Lautumiae gardens (p. 59)—but by "odeurs de vin suri, ruelles boueuses, puante échoppe où roulaient débardeurs, vagabonds, mariniers avinés."[1]

A similar irony envelops the recall, in the last section, of Michel's sensitivity to sensations of all kinds—that sensitivity which had played so large a part in the re-awakening of his senses at the beginning of the book. At that time, as a result of his eagerness to see, feel, hear and smell everything in nature which presented itself to his senses, a whole new world, and a hitherto unknown part of his being, were laid bare for his edification and enlightenment. But now, the servant has become the master, and the senses, unchecked, push Michel along the path to self-destruction. Ironically, the very phrases used provide a distant echo of similar passages in the first part: "J'épiais chaque bruit, d'une oreille plus attentive; je humais l'humidité de la nuit; je posais ma main sur des choses; je rôdais."[2] It is in the abrupt juxtaposition of the final phrase *je rôdais* that the full force of Gide's irony becomes apparent.

---

[1] *L'Immoraliste*, p. 171.   [2] *L'Immoraliste*, p. 169.

The example just given reinforces a point made earlier[1], that *L'Immoraliste* is in part a critical exposé of the dangers of excessive *disponibilité* and sympathy, two qualities which Gide himself possessed in rich abundance. Michel's power of sympathy with others is similarly parodied by an ironic confrontation of events in the first half of the work with events occurring in the second half. His active sympathy for health and beauty, as revealed early in the book by his attraction for robust native boys and Charles, the game-keeper's son, soon degenerates into a no less active, but debased, form of sympathy for ugliness and evil in the person of Alcide and other unsavoury characters. The extent to which Michel's power of sympathy has become distorted to serve unworthy ends is revealed, for example, by the pounding of his heart when Alcide is caught poaching ("j'apprends soudain l'affreuse volupté de celui qui braconne")[2], and, above all, in the revolting scene where he sleeps side by side with a group of Arabs in the street, returning home 'couvert de vermine' (p. 174).

What is achieved, in *L'Immoraliste*, through the very parallelism of the novel's structure, is achieved more subtly, in *La Porte étroite*, by an even more complex technique. This consists of an ironic juxtaposition of conflicting motives, as revealed in the two versions presented to the reader: that of Jérome's *récit* and that of Alissa's diary. Jérôme's non-comprehending version of the happenings is partly confirmed by Alissa's analysis of her successive states of mind, but just as firmly contradicted in many important points. Jérôme presents the mere façade, the outer appearance of reality—*le paraître*, while Alissa plumbs the hidden depths of the mind in an attempt to understand the true self—*l'être*. But further irony emerges from the very contradictions evident in the diary itself, from the clash between apparent motives and true motives in the mind of Alissa. It is above all by this device that Gide establishes, in the objective manner characteristic of him, the failure of Alissa's exalted quest for God.

Let us take one good example of this double-edged irony, arising from (a) discrepancies between Jérôme's account and Alissa's diary, and (b) contradictions within the text of the diary itself. Alissa has made up her mind to consummate her self-sacrifice, and has written to Jérôme, after one of their reunions at Fongueusemare, a letter of renunciation, which, however, Jérôme misinterprets, in his heady intoxication with the idea of virtue:—"Tout sentier, pourvu qu'il montât, me mènerait où la rejoindre. Ah! le terrain ne se rétrécirait jamais trop vite, pour ne supporter plus que nous deux!"[1] Yet, almost simultaneously, Alissa was revealing to her diary her own secret motives for her action, so radically opposed to Jérôme's reasoning. The almost identical nature of the image which she uses serves only to heighten the irony of this opposition: "Mais non! la route que vous nous enseignez, Seigneur, est une route étroite—étroite à n'y pouvoir marcher deux de front."[2] If Jérôme's fond illusions are destroyed, for the reader, by this relentless irony, it is equally true that our illusions of Alissa's unassailable strength are, in turn, shattered by her admission, a few pages later in the diary: "Mon Dieu, vous savez bien que j'ai besoin de lui (Jérôme) pour Vous aimer."[3] The vicious circle of this complex play of irony, and counter-irony, is thereby rendered complete.

Although the technique of *La Porte étroite* is more subtle than that of *L'Immoraliste*, as a result of this interplay between *récit* and diary, the nature of the irony revealed in each book offers striking similarities. As we have seen, Alissa, like Michel, suffers from delusions about the nature of her ideal. She deceives herself about the validity of her quest for God, as much as Michel deceives himself about the validity of his quest for the true self, and irony emerges from the discrepancy between real motives and false, between original intentions and the debasement of these intentions in actual practice. Thus, underlying Alissa's quest can be detected motives of false pride, vanity and even egotism, as inordinate in their way as the more obvious self-indulgence of Michel.

On the one hand, we have the outward appearance, the façade, of reality, as revealed by the events related by Jérôme. In particular, towards the end of the *récit*, we are presented with an image of Alissa which is all simplicity, humility and abasement of the self in the service of God. She has deliberately adopted a mode of hair-style and dress unbecoming to her, she is continually absorbed by humble, menial tasks and acts of charity, she has stripped her library of all works save "d'insignifiants petits ouvrages de piété vulgaire"—sermons and religious meditations written by "d'humbles âmes qui causent avec moi simplement". She warns Jérôme of the dangers of false pride, as seen in an author like Pascal, who, in the agonising uncertainty of his quest for God, appears to her to lose, rather than to gain, true faith: "'Qui veut

[1] *La Porte étroite*, p. 144.   [2] *Ibid.* p. 188.
[3] *Ibid.* p. 194.

sauver sa vie la perdra' ". Alissa appears, indeed, to have stripped herself of all pride and vanity, and to have opened her heart humbly to God, in accordance with her ideal, expressed in an earlier letter to Jérôme: "Mettre son ambition non à se révolter, mais à servir."[1]

Alissa's diary, however, permits us to peer behind the façade and to glimpse the real truth, which is quite different from these appearances. Ironically, Alissa is herself not free of the "orgueil abominable" with which, in the letter to Jérôme just quoted, she taxed the rebel seeking "une émancipation de la pensée". And, ironically again, the very phrase of Christ's which she quoted to condemn Pascal, can be turned round to incriminate her. By seeking to "save her life" i.e. by showing a too self-conscious zeal in her quest for faith, by ceaselessly analysing and questioning her motives instead of offering her heart simply and spontaneously to God, Alissa endangers, and indeed almost loses, her faith. Her motives, moreover, are not pure. She is lucid enough to discern, behind apparent motives, some of the real motives which inspire her actions. Just how disinterested was her initial sacrifice of herself for her sister, Juliette? The diary tells us: "je discerne bien qu'un affreux retour d'égoïsme s'offense de ce qu'elle ait trouvé son bonheur ailleurs que dans mon sacrifice— qu'elle n'ait pas eu besoin de mon sacrifice pour être heureuse."[2] Now that Juliette is happily married, her own sacrifice loses all its relevance. What is the origin of Alissa's consequent sense of humiliation save in feelings of vanity and wounded pride?

The diary shows further how, in her subsequent determination to continue her self-sacrifice, she is constantly beset by the temptations of false pride. Her act of renunciation has very little to do with real humility, and becomes partly an attempt to prove to herself that she was really capable of achieving it. It is a sense of pride in the nobility, and the uniqueness, of her undertaking, which urges her relentlessly onward and upward, even after she has lost sight of the goal which she has set herself: "Les raisons qui me font le fuir? Je n'y crois plus. . . Et je le fuis pourtant, avec tristesse, et sans comprendre pourquoi je le fuis."[3] So that the quest for God becomes the gratuitous pursuit of an heroic ideal, and, indeed, the pursuit of an exalted vision of *oneself*. The pride of Alissa here rejoins the similar pride of Michel. Significantly, even the simple act of tearing a few pages out of her diary, because, Alissa thought, they

[1] *La Porte étroite*, p. 110.
[2] *La Porte étroite*, pp. 179-80.   [3] *Ibid.* p. 187

revealed too great a preoccupation with style, is accompanied by a feeling of pride, which, however, she is lucid enough to detect within her mind: "Vraiment il semblait que j'eusse là du mérite et que ce que je supprimais fût grand'chose!"[1]

The irony of these contrasts between *récit* and diary allows us to substitute pride for humility as one of the chief motives underlying Alissa's behaviour. The irony of similar contrasts allows us to discern, beneath the apparent strength and uncompromising austerity of Alissa's attitude, a pathetically frail and uncertain human figure. As in the case of Michel, Allissa's weakness springs from her moving attachment to, and dependence on, the person she loves. The failure of the saint is the result of the same human weakness as the failure of the superman. But, were it not for the necessary corrective of Alissa's diary, our image of Alissa would be a very incomplete one. From Jérôme's account, we retain above all the impression of an extraordinary saintliness and austerity, and a great strength of mind, which will enable her to realise her exalted aims without ever deviating from the path she has chosen. But the true picture, as revealed in Alissa's diary, is a very different one—that of a tragic, heart-breaking uncertainty about herself and a love for Jérôme that no quest for virtue can succeed even in diminishing, let alone in suppressing. If Jérôme's narrative shows, by implication, his passive dependence on Alissa, the latter's diary brings home to the reader even more forcefully her tragic dependence on Jérôme. Page after page re-echoes with the same cry: "Existerais-je sans lui? Je ne suis qu'avec lui . . . Toute ma vertu n'est que pour lui plaire"[2]; "Il me semble à présent que je n'ai jamais 'tendu à la perfection' que pour lui."[3]; "Je n'ai goût qu'à ce qui l'intéresse, et ma pensée a pris la forme de la sienne au point que je ne sais les distinguer"[4]; "Mon Dieu, Vous savez bien que j'ai besoin de lui pour Vous aimer."[5]

By an even crueller irony, Gide has bestowed on Alissa the same sensual longings, the same physical desires which the latter subconsciously condemned in her mother, Lucile Bucolin. There is in Alissa not only a desire for spiritual communion with Jérôme, but a physical attraction as well, which, in spite of herself, she cannot suppress. One finds a significant passage in the diary, in which Jérôme is standing next to

---

[1] *La Porte étroite*, p. 188.   [2] *La Porte étroite*, p. 182.
[3] *Ibid.*, p. 185.   [4] *Ibid.*, pp. 188-9.
[5] *La Porte étroite*, p. 194.

Alissa and reading over her shoulder. She feels his breath and the warmth of his body, and at once her whole physical being responds involuntarily to his presence: "Je feignais de continuer ma lecture, mais je ne comprenais plus; je ne distinguais même plus les lignes; un trouble si étrange s'était emparé de moi que j'ai dû me lever de ma chaise, en hâte, tandis que je le pouvais encore."[1] By this deliberate irony, the image of an invulnerable and disembodied Alissa, such as emerges from Jérôme's *récit*, is effectively destroyed. As a result, she becomes a less idealised and a more human figure, one with whose inner contradictions we can actively sympathise. And the lesson for Alissa, as well as for Jérôme, is well summed up in these words of André Walter, which could serve admirably as a motto for the whole book: "Oui, vanité, la chasteté! Vanité — C'est un orgueil qui se déguise; pouvoir se croire supérieur, très noble au-dessus des autres... Si encore l'on triomphait: mais on ne supprime rien."[2]

By far the most bitter irony in *La Porte étroite* comes from the clash between the ideal of happiness in God, which Alissa ardently pursues, and the destiny of intolerable anguish and suffering which she actually achieves. A similar irony was observed in *L'Immoraliste*, where, as here, it was used to emphasise the utter failure of the hero's mission. In *La Porte étroite*, this is achieved by the revelation of inner contradictions within the text of Alissa's diary, by a tragic opposition between aims and achievements. One of Alissa's chief desires in her quest for God is the attainment of happiness, and not only happiness in an after-life, but one which she can enjoy in this world—ET NUNC. She has a distant presentiment of "cette joie radieuse" and realises that "toute (sa) vie est vaine sinon pour aboutir au bonheur."[3] But the cup of joy is dashed cruelly from her lips, leaving only bitter dregs of sadness and suffering. The cry *tristesse*, not *joie*, re-echoes fearfully throughout the last pages of Alissa's diary, recalling the similar disillusionment of Michel's final journey to Africa. Three successive entries in her diary reveal her unhappy state of mind: "Je le sens à *ma tristesse*, que le sacrifice n'est pas consommé dans mon cœur... A quelle médiocre, triste vertu je parviens!... A présent toute ma prière est plaintive... Cette parole si simple m'a plongée ce matin dans une tristesse dont rien ne pouvait me distraire."[4] The full irony of her earlier statement that "ce cahier doit

---

[1] *Ibid.*, p. 185.   [2] *André Walter*, p. 180.
[3] *La Porte étroite*, p. 201.   [4] *Ibid.*, p. 190-1.

m'aider à réobtenir en moi le bonheur,"[1] becomes now, in retrospect, only too apparent. Pascal, of whom Alissa had said: "La foi parfaite n'a pas tant de larmes ni de tremblement dans la voix"[2], here obtains his revenge, and irony turns the statement around upon its originator.

Not only does Alissa fail to achieve *le bonheur*, she also fails to achieve even a partial communion with her God, in spite of all her desperate efforts. This is the crowning irony of the whole book, and one which finally exposes the apparent futility of her self-sacrifice. Irony here is no simple literary device of contrast and juxtaposition, but assumes the proportions of a tragic conflict which stirs the very depths of the soul. Who can read the last poignant pages of Alissa's diary without becoming personally involved in her distress: "Seigneur! Je crie à Vous de toutes mes forces. Je suis dans la nuit; j'attends l'aube. Je crie à Vous jusqu'à mourir."[3]; or without sharing in the sense of bitter defeat which marks her last anguished moments on earth: "une angoisse s'est emparée de moi, un frisson de la chair et de l'âme; c'était comme l'*éclaircissement* brusque et désenchanté de ma vie. Il me semblait que je voyais pour la première fois les murs atrocement nus de ma chambre. J'ai pris peur. . . Je voudrais mourir à présent, vite, avant d'avoir compris de nouveau que je suis seule."[4]

★   ★   ★

Style

The technique of the first-person narrator implies, on the part of the author, some effort to reveal the character of the hero not only by what he says but also by his manner of saying it—in other words, the style is to be a revelation of the character himself, in the same way as it is normally a revelation of the author. For a writer with an ardent desire for objectivity, here is yet another way in which he may achieve the illusion of detachment and present his fictional world as a completely independent creation, existing in its own right. Since Gide, in both *L'Immoraliste* and *La Porte étroite*, has sought to adapt his style to that of the narrator —with varying degrees of success, as we shall see—any examination of the technique of these stories would be incomplete without reference

[1] *Ibid.*, p. 180.   [2] *Ibid.*, p. 153.
[3] *Ibid.*, p. 201.   [4] *La Porte étroite*, pp. 201-2.

to their style, for the light which it sheds both on the chief characters and on the writer himself.

In general, the writing of *L'Immoraliste* represents a true landmark in the development of Gide's style. It is, indeed, difficult to believe that this *récit* was written by the same hand which, ten years earlier, had produced so curious a work as *Les Cahiers d'André Walter*. With few writers can a mere decade have brought about so complete a transformation in their attitude to composition and style. In 1891, Gide, at once seeking a personnal manner of expression for the highly original ideas fermenting within him and obsessed with the desire to "étonner ses contemporains",[1] resorted to a tortuous and complicated style which later he would have been glad to disown. Elaborate and highly artificial images, a variety of complex rhythms, now smooth-flowing, now broken, in the approved Symbolist manner, arbitrary dislocations of syntax ("quand la syntaxe proteste, il la faut mater, la rétive")[2]—all these combine to give a dated air to much of Gide's very early work and to create an atmosphere which some readers may be justified in finding *irrespirable*. Gradually, however, as the last decade of the 19th century progresses, Gide comes to realise that "le triomphe de l'individualisme est dans le renoncement à l'individualité",[3] and, from that time onward, the great classical artist will slowly emerge. It is only when, according to his own admission, he fully understood the value of discipline, in submitting himself to the established rules of the French language, instead of seeking to bend it to his will, that the sober classicism of a work like *L'Immoraliste* became possible. In Professor Brée's words, "des classiques, il adopte le souci d'une langue précise, savamment travaillée, subordonnée à l'effet d'ensemble que doit donner l'œuvre,"[4] and the same critic quotes a letter written by Gide at this very period, which shows strikingly the writer's growing concern for precision and clarity: "Cette exigence toujours plus méchante vis-à-vis de moi-même, me fait reprendre huit fois la même phrase, et rester dessus une demi-journée, souvent pour la raturer le lendemain, cela pour des subtilités de décence, d'ordre ou de clarté, de rythme si ténues que je crains bien d'y être le seul sensible."[5]

The question of style, in a story involving the 'first-person narrator'

[1] *Incidences* (1948 edition) p. 38. [2] *André Walter*, p. 140.
[3] *Incidences*, p. 38. [4] G. Brée, *A. Gide*, p.185.
[5] Letter to Raymond Bonheur (12th March, 1900).

technique, poses difficult problems for a novelist who is anxious both to preserve a classical detachment from his characters and at the same time to safeguard the artistic value of his work. The two are not necessarily compatible, unless the hero–narrator happens also to be a talented literary artist capable of imparting real stylistic and dramatic qualities to his *récit*, which is not the case with either Michel or Jérôme. Three courses are then open to the writer: he may choose to neglect verisimilitude and write in a style which is not that of the narrator but which preserves true literary values, or else, going to the other extreme, he may throw overboard any exalted notion of style and art, and opt for credibility, writing in a manner which corresponds strictly to the character and mood of the narrator. A third solution—a compromise solution, also suggests itself: to adopt a style which respects, in its broad outlines, the character of the narrator, but which will constantly vary and fluctuate to harmonise with the lyrical and dramatic movement of the *récit*.

It is characteristic of Gide—never a man of extremes—that the compromise solution should appeal to him in the case of the two works we are considering, although, as we shall see, the pendulum swings more in the first direction, with *L'Immoraliste*, and in the second, with *La Porte étroite*. Why neither of the extreme courses could be envisaged by Gide should be obvious to those with a clear understanding of his attitude to art. In the first place, for Gide, style does not exist in a vacuum, it must always have a close relationship with the subject matter, and to ignore completely the figure of the narrator, which he has himself interposed between the reader and the author, by imposing on the subject his own style, would only have recalled the worst arrogances of the exponents of *L'Art pour l'Art*. Much as he was preoccupied with *le beau style*, what he sought was not style for its own sake, but the style which illuminates its subject, which grows naturally out of the theme or mood it is endeavouring to express. From the very outset of his career, Gide remained firm on this point, even though the style of his earliest works seemed to deny the principle in practice: "Que jamais le mot ne précède l'idée. . . Que le mot soit toujours nécessité par elle;"[1] "L'artiste, le savant, ne doit pas se préférer à la Vérité qu'il veut dire. . . ni le mot, ni la phrase, à l'idée qu'ils veulent montrer."[2]

The other extreme solution must have proved equally unacceptable

---

[1] *Journal* (31 Dec. 1891), p. 28.
[2] *Traité du Narcisse*, p. 8. (Pléiade edition).

to Gide, for to ignore entirely the demands of art, and to write in a style which should at every point be recognisable as the voice of the narrator, would certainly lead to authenticity, but would make the artist guilty of the worst excesses of the Realist-Naturalist writers, whom Gide so much despised. For him, as for every great writer, art is not the literal reproduction of reality, but the transformation of it into a superior form of reality, which corresponds to the artist's particular vision of the world. Without this unique vision, there is no art worthy of the name, only a slavish imitation of the external world.

In *L'Immoraliste*, then, let us not expect a style which will reproduce exactly the voice of Michel. If we demanded strict authenticity, we might ask Gide how it is that an archaeologist without especial literary pretensions, however brilliant he might be, could relate his story in a style so rich in literary merit, so full of excellent lyrical and dramatic qualities and containing such a wealth of suggestive images. Or we might wonder how a man so disillusioned and broken in spirit as Michel appears to be, could rise at times to such lyrical heights as does the narrator in telling his story to the friends who have come to rescue him. Michel's tone is not always strictly in harmony either with his professional interests or with the mood of extreme dejection in which he appears before his friends. To accuse Gide here of implausibility might savour of *chicanerie*, had not the author himself cast doubts on the literary capacities of Michel by writing to a friend: "Non, je ne pense pas que Michel puisse jamais écrire. Sa chaleur, vous le sentez bien, n'est qu'ardeur; elle brûle sans réchauffer; les mots se friperaient sous sa plume. Croyez bien, cher Scheffer, que ce n'est que parce que je ne suis pas Michel que j'ai pu raconter son histoire aussi 'remarquablement bien' que vous dites."[1]

This statement of Gide's sets the tone for the attitude he was to adopt towards Michel as narrator, and which we, in our turn, are surely justified in adopting. While resorting to a style which, in its essentials, is true to Michel's character and even, in general, to the mood of desolation and distress in which we find him, Gide has acknowledged the inability of the narrator to express adequately the great lyrical and dramatic moments of the story, and it is then that Gide, the great writer and stylist, has visibly taken over the narrative himself. Thus, there is, in *L'Immoraliste*, not one, but several styles, each corresponding to the ebb and flow of the varying moods of the story—in turn concise, brief

---

[1] Quoted by Lafille, p. 8.

and terse, even to the point of cruelty, yet eloquent, lyrical and dramatic at the great moments of climax. In accordance with Gide's artistic principles, and in his own memorable phrase, "la phrase est une excroissance de l'idée".[1] The result is a style both varied and rich, a style which Professor Brée describes as possessing "une luminosité, une beauté étudiée, . . . que Gide ne retrouvera pas lorsqu'il tentera de rendre ses personnages entièrement autonomes."[2]

Much of Michel's story is told in the terse, clipped, uncompromising style of a man who, like many scholars, is not given to verbiage, one whose language is as precise as his thought. Such a tone is at the same time appropriate to the general mood of disillusionment and apathetic indifference in which we find Michel at the beginning of the story. Here is a man for whom life has lost all its lustre, and who, in spite of the compulsive urge he feels to tell his story, is in no mood for eloquence or artistic embroidery: "Marceline était très jolie. Vous le savez; vous l'avez vue. Je me reprochai de ne m'en être pas d'abord aperçu. Je la connaissais trop pour la voir avec nouveauté; nos familles de tout temps étaient liées; je l'avais vue grandir; j'étais habitué à sa grâce."[3] "Nous nous assîmes sur un banc. Marceline se taisait. Des Arabes passèrent; puis survint une troupe d'enfants. Marceline en connaissait plusieurs et leur fit signe; ils s'approchèrent."[4]

But, at other times, usually at the great climactic points of the story, the style develops a passionate intensity, a lyrical movement, which, while hardly appropriate to the broken-spirited, apathetic figure who is now telling his story, nevertheless remains, in spirit, true to the feelings which Michel must have experienced at the time of his profound reawakening to life. The style remains true to the essential spirit, if not to the letter, in such a moving passage as the following, where Marceline reassures Michel about his eventual recovery from the illness which has prostrated him: "Mais, aussitôt, elle me répondit:—Tu guériras!—avec une conviction si passionnée que, presque convaincu moi-même, j'eus comme un confus sentiment de tout ce que la vie pouvait être, de son amour à elle, la vague vision de si pathétiques beautés, que les larmes jaillirent de mes yeux et que je pleurais longuement sans pouvoir ni vouloir m'en défendre."[5] And if the real Michel would hardly seem

[1] *Journal* ("Littérature et Morale"), p. 94, Pléiade edition.
[2] G. Brée, *A. Gide*, p. 178.   [3] *L'Immoraliste*, p. 18.
[4] *Ibid.*, p. 39.   [5] *L'Immoraliste*, p. 25.

capable of so suggestive and eloquent a metaphor as the following, should we not accept it in the spirit in which it was intended, as conveying a vivid, but true, image of the Michel of that particular moment, overflowing with a rich, new sense of life: "Il y avait ici. . . l'afflux d'un sang plus riche et plus chaud qui devait toucher mes pensées, les toucher une à une, pénétrer tout, émouvoir, colorer les plus lointaines, délicates et secrètes fibres de mon être."[1]

This last example is typical, in general, of the style of *L'Immoraliste*, where the expression is intimately wedded to the dramatic movement of the story—a requirement which Flaubert, ever since *Madame Bovary*, has led us to demand of any great novel. André Walter laid it down as an essential principle for the form of the novel he was planning to write, in which he insisted that "le rythme des phrases. . . ondule, selon la courbe des pensées cadencées, par une corrélation subtile."[2] In *L'Immoraliste*, Gide has generally respected this principle, varying his style in accordance with the dramatic fluctuations of the story and conveying, by syntax and image, the constantly changing emotions or states of mind. Thus, during the first days of Michel's serious illness, the rhythm of the style conveys vividly the feverish weakness of the patient. "Marceline est auprès de moi. Elle lit; elle coud; elle écrit. Je ne fais rien. Je la regarde. O Marceline! Marceline!. . . Je regarde. Je vois le soleil; je vois l'ombre; je vois la ligne de l'ombre se déplacer; j'ai si peu à penser, que je l'observe. Je suis encore très faible; je respire très mal; tout me fatigue, même lire."[3] Later, as strength slowly returns to him, and the couple journey back through Italy, Michel is able to take longer and longer walks. Here, as Michel tries out his new-found strength, once more the movement of the style closely coincides with the successive sensations experienced by the hero: "Pourtant les escaliers ne m'exténuaient plus; je m'exerçais à les gravir la bouche close; j'espaçais toujours plus mes haltes, me disais: j'irai jusque-là sans faiblir; puis, arrivé au but, trouvant dans mon orgueil content ma récompense, je respirais longuement, puissamment, et de façon qu'il me semblât sentir l'air pénétrer plus efficacement ma poitrine."[4] Who cannot sense, in the very structure of the first half of this sentence, with its breathless spacings and pauses, Michel's superhuman effort to climb the stairs, then, as the goal is reached, the welcome *détente* and sense of relief, expressed by the more ample and eloquent

[1] *Ibid.*, p. 60.   [2] *André Walter*, p. 97.
[3] *L'Immoraliste*, p. 28.   [4] *Ibid.*, pp. 62-3.

rhythm of the second half, and by the powerful exhalation of the adverbs *longuement, puissamment, efficacement?*

At the more dramatic moments of the story, such as when Michel returns home to Marceline's bedside to find all the frightening evidence of her miscarriage, the style conveys by its anguished movement the emotions of the hero. What more striking expression of Michel's sudden panic than the very form of this sentence: "je vis des instruments luisants, de l'ouate; je vis, crus voir, un linge taché de sang. . . Je sentis que je chancelais. Je tombai presque vers le docteur; il me soutint. Je comprenais; j'avais peur de comprendre."[1] A dramatic brevity or terseness of style is particularly evident in the account of Michel's last fatal journey to Africa with Marceline, where the breathless speed of the narration matches the inhuman, relentless speed of the journey itself. A variation here is the narrator's use of a device which gives even greater vividness to the story. Reverting to the present tense, he relates the events as though they were occurring for the first time before his very eyes, so that he notes down his surprised reactions to the events *as they take place*. The resulting dramatic effect is sometimes quite startling, as in the scene where the repentant Michel fills the apartment with flowers as a surprise for Marceline: "Déjà je me réjouis de sa joie. Je l'entends venir. La voici. Elle ouvre la porte. Qu'a-t-elle?. . . Elle chancelle. . . Elle éclate en sanglots."[2] And how appropriately the broken syntax of the following sentence expresses Michel's angry reaction to Marceline's refusal of the flowers: "Sans rien dire, je saisis ces innocentes branches fragiles, les brise, les emporte, les jette, exaspéré, le sang aux yeux."[3]

The very images used by Michel also testify to the author's belief that the "word" should always be necessitated by the "idea", for they are always appropriate either to the character of the narrator or to the mood and atmosphere of a particular moment in the story. Such an image is the elaborate palimpsest symbol (pp. 59-60), so exactly in harmony with Michel's archaeological interests, and which has been well analysed in Professor Ullman's book *The Image in the Modern French Novel*. There is no need to add further to Professor Ullman's already complete survey[4] of the images employed in *L'Immoraliste*, except to point out two examples where both the structure of the style and the

---

[1] *L'Immoraliste*, p. 126.
[2] *Ibid.*, p. 167. For a further example of this *procédé*, cf. p. 175.
[3] *Ibid.*, p. 168. [4] cf. pp. 23-30.

image itself harmonise closely with the atmosphere of a moment in the story. The period of respite, of calm, in Michel's *récit*, as Marceline awaits the arrival of her child at La Morinière, is evoked by a placid image and further reflected in the smooth-flowing eloquence of the style: "Comme un souffle parfois plisse une eau très tranquille, la plus légère émotion sur son front se laissait lire; en elle, mystérieusement elle écoutait frémir une nouvelle vie; je me penchais sur elle comme sur une profonde eau pure, où, si loin qu'on voyait, on ne voyait que de l'amour."[1] An entirely different impression—an impression, indeed, of decadence and decay, is conveyed by Michel's later description of *la maison Heurtevent* as "un lieu brûlant, à l'odeur forte, autour duquel, malgré que j'en eusse, mon imagination, comme une mouche à viande, tournoyait"[2]. Here, to quote Professor Ullmann's analysis, "the unpleasant quality of the. . . image is effectively underlined by the syntax which, by its halts and parentheses, pictures Michel's curiosity restlessly circling around the unwholesome place."[3]

In spite, however, of Gide's efforts in *L'Immoraliste* to adopt the style of his narrator or to vary the expression in accordance with the changing moods of the story, the style retains much of the characteristic Gidean flavour, so that we do not have to read far before words, expressions or whole sentences bearing the unmistakeable stamp of the author come to light. The great stylist can never conceal himself for long in an alien form, even when, as in *La Porte étroite*, he was to make even more determined efforts to submerge his own personality beneath the identity of his hero. What more Gidean than the ring of sentences like "j'usais dans le travail une ferveur singulière" (p. 16); "je devais faire de la vie la palpitante découverte" (p. 27)? Or the slightly *précieux* flavour of the lyricism in the following image: "Ah! je voudrais qu'en chaque phrase, ici, toute une moisson de volupté se distille" (p. 173); or the highly literary inversion of subject and verb in: "plus voluptueusement se présentait à nous chaque instant, plus insensiblement coulait l'heure." (p. 83)? Throughout the *Immoraliste*, we find Gide's predilection for such inversions, especially the placing of adjectives before nouns for literary effect, as in "les reflets dans les dormantes eaux" (p. 81); his fondness for the somewhat rarefied *j'eusse* construction (instead of *j'aurais*) (cf. pp. 102-3), and for imperfect subjunctives of the type *souffrissent*,

---

[1] *L'Immoraliste*, p. 98.　[2] *Ibid.*, p. 141.
[3] *op. cit.*, p. 29.

contraignissent, s'amusassent (p. 134); his love of words used in a sense somewhat removed from their normal sense, like *attente* (p. 53), *pertuis* (for *trou*, p. 143), or of expressive words which he has not hesitated to coin for his own use, like *illimitait* (p. 134). Such turns bear the imprint of the authentic Gide.

No less authentic, and unmistakeable, is the narrator's frequent use of the ternary rhythm, a *procédé* dear to the heart of Gide. One is aware of Chateaubriand's predilection for this rhythm, but it is above all to Flaubert that Gide seems indebted for its use—Flaubert who had been, at the beginning of his career, Gide's great master in rhythm and style, and whose *Correspondance* was at the age of twenty his *livre de chevet*. Certain sentences in *L'Immoraliste*, indeed, evoke a rhythm with which all lovers of Flaubert are only too familiar: "Sous le soleil, ardent déjà, des buées s'élevaient; l'oasis fumait tout entière; on entendait gronder au loin l'Oued débordé."[1] And, as again in Flaubert, the ternary rhythm may produce either the effect of lyrical and oratorical flow or that of abruptness, the corrective to eloquence. Consider the appropriateness to the sense of the following *coupes*: "Je l'écoutai; je l'épiai; je le sentis."[2] (Michel fighting determinedly against the inner foe, the illness which has prostrated him); "Je rôdais, je suivais, j'épiais."[3] (Michel's growing fascination for evil, in all its various forms). But when it is a question of evoking the luminous, transparent clarity of the air around Tunis, the ternary rhythm flows with all the smoothness and liquidity of the light itself: "L'air lui-même semble un fluide lumineux où tout baigne, où l'on plonge, où l'on nage."[4] And how noticeably the ternary rhythm of the following sentences adds to the eloquence, to the lyrical flow of the passage as a whole: "Là des menthes croissaient, odorantes; *j'en* cueillis, *j'en froissai* les feuilles, *j'en frottai* tout mon corps humide, mais brûlant. Je me regardai *longuement, sans plus de honte aucune, avec joie.* Je me trouvais, non pas robuste encore, mais pouvant l'être, *harmonieux, sensuel, presque beau.*"[5] This passage, at the end of a chapter, like so many of the eloquent passages of *L'Immoraliste* (showing Gide's concern as an artist for polished perfection of form), is a veritable harvest of ternaries, in which not only verbs, but also adjectives, adverbs and adverbial phrases present themselves in

---

[1] *L'Immoraliste*, p. 53.   [2] *L'Immoraliste*, p. 32.
[3] *Ibid.*, p. 134.   [4] *Ibid.*, p. 174.
[5] *L'Immoraliste*, p. 65; underlinings mine.

cascading groups of three. With Gide, however, this is no technique of *l'art pour l'art*, or *le beau style* for its own sake, but a form of expression constantly in harmony with the thought.

La Porte étroite has very little of the variety and richness of style which is to be found in *L'Immoraliste*. It is significant that Professor Ullmann has found in the later book a considerable reduction in the number of images used, which is part of a general tendency in Gide's style towards an ever greater *dépouillement* and simplicity of line. This is, however, only part of the story, for, in *La Porte étroite*, the comparative bareness of expression is largely due to a conscious effort on the part of Gide to place himself "within the skin" of the narrator and to render faithfully the character of Jérôme by a deliberately flat, and somewhat colourless style.[1] Thus Gide's attempt at greater realism in *La Porte étroite* leads inevitably to a sacrifice in artistic effect, and from the rich multiplicity of styles characteristic of *L'Immoraliste*, we are reduced to the more sober unity of a single style—or rather, of two styles, that of Jérôme and that of Alissa. Gide has, indeed, been very careful to distinguish between the widely differing styles of Jérôme and Alissa, and we can only concur in his own personal view that the real artistic success of the book is to be found in the language of Alissa's letters and diary. Simple, unadorned, natural and, at times, profoundly moving in its simplicity, the style of Alissa provides a striking contrast to the more mediocre and uninspiring narrative of Jérôme.

Re-reading *La Porte étroite* some time later, Gide could not help being struck by the poverty of the expression in Jérôme's *récit*. This, as he well realised, was the price to be paid for greater realism, "le flasque caractère de mon Jérôme impliquant la flasque prose".[2] He considered the style as being "très digne assurément du morne caractère du héros", but claimed that, given the special nature of his intentions, it could hardly have been otherwise: "je crois ... que j'étais contraint, parlant à la première personne indispensablement, de parler ainsi et que par ses défauts mêmes, le livre est réussi; mais combien cette réussite dans la veulerie m'est déplaisante!"[3] Jérôme's style is, indeed, a faithful reflection of his character—at times, flat, lifeless and banal, at other times, pretentious, artificial, affected and slightly unctuous. Devoid of

---

[1] cf. the parallel case of Meursault, the narrator of Camus' *L'Etranger*.

[2] *Journal* (1909), p. 276.

[3] Letter to A.R. (1909), quoted by Lafille, p. 37.

real literary talent and well aware himself of what he describes as "mon médiocre lyrisme" (p. 52), he is quite adequate to the task of narrator so long as he remains within his limits, but let him venture beyond these limits into the realms of creative style or metaphor, and the effect is nearly always *manqué*, if not disastrous. It is then that we have the conventional banality of images like: "un matin que l'air charmant riait et que notre cœur s'ouvrait comme les fleurs,"[1] and, "tout mon bonheur ouvrait les ailes, s'échappait de moi vers les cieux."[1] Or the tone may become stilted, *précieux*, even intolerably artificial, as in the following examples: "la joie et la santé posaient sur (Juliette) leur éclat;"[2] "je pressais sa tête contre mon cœur et sur son front mes lèvres par où mon âme s'écoulait"[3]; "(je) laissais tomber à terre ses paroles comme de pauvres oiseaux blessés."[4] At other times, Jérôme appears to be carried away by the impressive sound of his own voice, and his utterance becomes pretentious, pompous, even unctuous: "Je me défendais mal contre une si flatteuse chaleur, m'en sentais enfin pénétré et cédais doucement à l'attrait de ses propositions chimériques".[5] "A présent que je mesure la force de votre amour à la ruse de son silence et à sa cruelle industrie, dois-je vous aimer d'autant plus que vous m'aurez plus atrocement désolé?"[6]

Gide's constant fidelity, in the style of *La Porte étroite*, to the character of the narrator, constituted a remarkable *tour de force* which left the author in a state bordering on exhaustion. At the same time, the highly complex technique of the book, with its alternating succession of *récit*, letters and diary, enabled him to avoid the ever-present danger of monotony inherent in a technique of presentation from a single point of view. Gide has achieved variety, while presenting, in the style of the narrative, a faithful image of Jérôme—so faithful, indeed, that the one occasion when he violates this principle, in the latter half of chapter 4, is merely the exception which proves the rule. We shall be analysing this episode in a later section. Suffice it to say for the present that, in chapter 4, where Jérôme, for perhaps the first and only time, reveals a sensitivity to literary values by presenting dramatic events in a highly dramatic manner, the style is unique by its conciseness, vividness and speed of movement. If this is a style which we can hardly

---

[1] *La Porte étroite*, p. 141.   [2] *Ibid.*, p. 20.
[3] *Ibid.*, p. 24.   [4] *Ibid.*, p. 54.
[5] *La Porte étroite*, p. 73.   [6] *Ibid.*, pp. 146-7.

reconcile with what we know of Jérôme's character and literary talents, at least the loss in psychological truth is compensated by a corresponding gain in dramatic tension.

In general, then, we can say that Jérôme's narration of the events in *La Porte étroite* has more the authentic ring of his personality than is the case with the narrator of *L'Immoraliste*. Yet, even here the voice of Gide rings out clearly in many an expressive phrase or sentence. Favourite Gidean words like *attente*, or coined words, pregnant with meaning, such as *inespérément* (p. 49), *dépoétisation* (p. 149 and p. 160), *orientalement* ("le ciel était orientalement pur", p. 65), are sprinkled throughout the text. What more Gidean than the persuasive sonorities of a sentence like the following: "L'été, cette année, fut splendide. Tout semblait pénétré d'azur. Notre ferveur triomphait du mal, de la mort; l'ombre reculait devant nous. Chaque matin j'étais éveillé par ma joie; je me levais dès l'aurore, à la rencontre du jour m'élançais ..."[1] or the characteristic ternary rhythm of "ne concevant plus d'autre but à ma vie que d'abriter cette enfant contre la peur, contre le mal, contre la vie."[2]? Even the style of Alissa, so different in its essential spirit from that of Jérôme, at times evokes unmistakeable echoes of the authentic Gide, as in the ternaries and the final displacement of the adverb in the following passage from one of her letters: "Oh! qu'il soit fini pour jamais, cet affreux hiver de silence! Depuis que te voilà retrouvé, *la vie, la pensée, notre âme*, tout me paraît *beau, adorable, fertile* inépuisablement ..."[3]

To sum up, our preference for the style of either *L'Immoraliste* or *La Porte étroite* will depend on our attitude to art. If we prefer verisimilitude, it will be found in Gide's attempt to reproduce faithfully in the style the platitudinous accents of Jérôme and the stark natural simplicity of Alissa. If we prefer that art should transform reality into something finer, purer and nobler than mere representation, in short, that art should transcend reality, then we shall inevitably choose the rich variety, the lyrical and dramatic movement, of Michel's style, without questioning possible lapses from authenticity.

---

[1] *La Porte étroite*, p. 47. [2] *Ibid.*, p. 24.
[3] *Ibid.*, p. 111. Underlinings mine.

CHAPTER THREE

Structure

Structure and Symbolism

Any examination of the structure of *L'Immoraliste* and *La Porte étroite* must necessarily be preceded by a discussion of the *genre* to which they belong. Are they novels, or are they *récits*, as Gide in fact described them? And what is to be understood by a *récit*? Our answers to these questions will determine our attitude to the technique of composition displayed in each work.

First, it should be noted that Gide refused to consider them as novels and objected to those critics who found them lacking in qualities more appropriate to a novel. For him, a novel was a much more ambitious project than a *récit*, and one, in fact, which he consciously undertook only once in his life, some years later, when he wrote *Les Faux-Monnayeurs*. "Le roman, tel que je le reconnais ou l'imagine, comporte une diversité de points de vue soumise à la diversité des personnages qu'il met en scène; c'est par essence une œuvre déconcentrée."[1] If "deconcentration" was, for Gide, the essence of the novel, the distinguishing feature of the *récit* was, on the contrary, compression or concentration. Instead of several points of view, we have one single view, that of the narrator (or two, in the case of *La Porte étroite*); instead of a diversity of characters, we have a very small number, each of them gravitating around, and throwing light on, one principal character (Michel and Alissa). The hero (or heroine) occupies the centre of the stage, with the spotlight constantly focussed on him, and the whole book is but the development of a single theme, the account of a crisis in the life of the hero. Enough has been said to indicate the essentially *dramatic* conception of the Gidean *récit*, which, in turn, entails a certain sacrifice of complexity, a simplifying of the general outline, structure and characterisation of the work.

It will also be seen how closely this type of *récit* approximates to the form of fiction known as the *nouvelle*. All that has just been said about the *récit* can apply equally well to the *nouvelle*. However, they differ in two important respects—firstly, in length, and secondly, as regards

[1] Quoted by Lafille, p. 63.

the duration of the actual events recorded. A *nouvelle* is usually short in length, hardly ever exceeding 100 pages. At the same time, it is often (but not always[1]) the account of one highly significant, but isolated episode. From this point of view, *L'Immoraliste* and *La Porte étroite* offer examples of a *genre* midway between the *nouvelle* and the *roman*. They are as long as novels, and the plot of each work extends over a longer period of time than does the single, significant episode of the *nouvelle*. Yet they lack the complexity of true novels. Paul Bourget's definition of the two extremes of *roman* and *nouvelle* may serve to indicate the intermediary position occupied by the Gidean *récit*:

"(Le roman) procède par développement, la nouvelle par concentration. Les épisodes du roman peuvent être tout menus, insignifiants presque ... L'épisode traité par la nouvelle doit être intensément significatif. Le roman permet, il commande la diversité du ton ... La nouvelle exige l'unité du coloris, peu de touches, mais qui conspirent à un effet unique ... Elle est un *solo*. Le roman est une symphonie."[2] If this last analogy is valid, may it be possible to characterise the *récit* as a kind of "concerto", in which the hero represents the solo instrument?

L'Immoraliste and *La Porte étroite* each show but single aspects of the authors' personality, whereas *Les Faux-Monnayeurs*, like any novel worthy of the name, attempts to "communicate a whole world, represent (the) author's entire vision, orchestrate all the parts of his imagination."[3] In Gide's own words, the novel is to be *une somme*, with a multiplicity of characters and themes interweaving through the complex fabric of its structure (one critic who has undertaken the thankless task of counting them, can distinguish, in *Les Faux-Monnayeurs*, as many as 40 different characters and 50 different themes!) Far from presenting the well-rounded contours of the typical Gidean *récit*, it seeks to render faithfully the complexity of life itself, which, in Bergsonian terms, is a *durée*, in perpetual movement or *devenir*, without the artificial beginning and end that certain writers would impose on it. Hence the apparent shapelessness of the novel, the impression it gives of beginning afresh with each chapter and the air of non-finality created at the end of the work: "Pourrait être continué: c'est sur ces mots que je voudrais

[1] Cf, for example, Mérimée's *Carmen*.

[2] P. Bourget, "Mérimée nouvelliste", *Revue des deux mondes*, 15 September 1920, p. 263.

[3] J. Hytier, *André Gide* (Howard translation), p. 125.

terminer mes *Faux-Monnayeurs*." Hence, also, the impression of a continuous and ever changing creation, as though the novelist is swept along irresistibly by the fast-flowing current of life: "Le romancier traduit la vie au moment où elle se fait, il en exprime fidèlement les sinuosités et le rythme, son intelligence paraît dirigée plutôt que directrice."[1]

As we have seen, the greater concentration of the *récit* inevitably leads to some simplification in the general structure of the book, as well as in the presentation of the characters. We can express this in terms of the symbolic qualities of the work. All literature is symbolic—this is the necessary condition of its existence. For an artist, one obsessed with perfection of form, as was Gide, the *raison suffisante*, the symbol, of the work, was its structure and composition: "Une œuvre bien composée est nécessairement symbolique. Autour de quoi viendraient se grouper les parties? qui guiderait leur ordonnance? sinon l'idée de l'œuvre, qui fait cette ordonnance symbolique."[2] If, as W. Tindall defined it, a symbol is the outward sign of an inward state, the work of art is the outward and concrete manifestation of an idea pre-existing in the imagination of the author. Thus, developing Gide's statement, the idea of the work will necessarily dictate the form in which it is expressed, and the form should aspire to becoming the perfect expression, the perfect symbol, of the idea. It is perhaps misleading here to talk of 'idea', for it may be not only a single theme (as in Gide's *récits* or in certain novels conceived according to more unified dramatic principles), but indeed a multiplicity of intersecting themes, as in the great historical frescoes like *War and Peace*. Let us speak rather of the *Idea* of the work of art. However complex this latter may be, the form of the work should be completely conditioned by it, so that all the diverse elements which enter into its composition—structure, plot, background, characters and style—all inevitably lead back, however indirectly, to the central Idea, or, as with a prism, reflect its many

[1] R. Fernandez, *Messages*, p. 64. One could hardly make this claim for Gide in writing *Les Faux-Monnayeurs*. On the contrary, one is forever conscious of a lucid critical intelligence which never relaxes its control during the process of artistic composition. Nowhere does one gain the impression of *vie débordante* which inspires the creations of a Balzac. Gide, one is forced to conclude, is a novelist of considerable talent rather than a novelist of true genius.

[2] *Journal* (1896), *Littérature et morale*, p. 94 (Pléiade edition).

varying facets. It is this which, for Gide, as for a great artist like Flaubert, constitutes the intrinsic unity of a work of art.

Any discussion of novel technique sooner or later brings us to *Madame Bovary*. What makes this novel the great masterpiece that it is, is the extent to which its form is the perfect representation of the Idea. Every element in this work—situations, people, background and style— becomes a signpost pointing in the direction of Flaubert's central theme: the disparity between Illusion and Reality, between the ideal world of our dreams and the cruel world of every-day life. More than that—the slightest incident, the most commonplace object, becomes invested with a magical symbolic power, a force of poetic suggestion which not only evokes the main theme in the immediate context but expands beyond, by a sort of infinite radiation, into a perceptive vision of life itself. It is in this sense that, as Conrad said, "all the great creations of literature have been symbolic, and in that way have gained in complexity, in power, in depth and in beauty."[1] *Madame Bovary* is, from this point of view, an artistic *tour de force*, comprising a veritable network of poetic symbols which subtly lead in all directions at once—to one another, to the central theme, or, going beyond the text, towards a richer vision of life. Dr. Fairlie, in her penetrating study of *Madame Bovary*,[2] has shown how the most trivial incidents or details may assume, as a result of these subtle interrelationships, a significance far greater than their intrinsic value.[3] The use of poetic symbolism adds, to the literal meaning of a scene or object, not one, but a multiplicity of symbolic meanings.

It is too much to expect that the simpler form of the *récit*, as Gide conceived of it, should take on the rich, almost infinite power of suggestion which we find in a complex novel like *Madame Bovary*. Nevertheless, symbolism plays an important part both in *L'Immoraliste* and *La Porte étroite*. Its effect is visible on the structure, the characterisation and the backgrounds of both works, and it manifests itself in the form of symmetrical patterns sometimes imposed artificially on the text. In particular, in *L'Immoraliste*, Gide has exposed himself to the danger of simplification of structure which is inherent in the *récit* form. In other words, far from achieving the subtlety and complexity found in the symbolic patterns of *Madame Bovary*, he has made the structure of

[1] Quoted by W. Tindall, *The Literary Symbol*, p. 87.
[2] No. 8 in this series.   [3] cf. especially, *op. cit.*, pp. 35-7.

L'Immoraliste a too obvious symbol of the Idea of the work, one which is too easily reducible to a symbolic graph or an algebraic equation. The infinitely "expanding" symbols of *Madame Bovary* are here replaced by more static symbols, by a more rigid, more artificial formalism and symmetry, which, although cleverly used to illustrate certain dramatic parallels and contrasts within the body of the work, deprive it of the complexity one would expect to find in the structure of a true novel. On the other hand, the *récit* takes on an admirable logic, clarity and purity of line which help to compensate for this loss of complexity.

(a) *Structure of Plot*

The basic Idea of *L'Immoraliste* is the awakening and development of the individual self and the conflict this produces in the life of the couple. Marceline must "decrease" so that Michel may "increase". This theme is expressed in the very structure of the book by a series of symmetrical patterns and contrasts. Part III is Part I in reverse. Part I shows us an ailing Michel gradually gaining strength as he progresses north from Africa through Italy to France, a recovery which is accompanied by a growing feeling of joy and exaltation as he re-discovers life. At the begining, Michel's health is weak and Marceline's is strong. ("Marceline, au contraire, semblait robuste"—p. 17). In Part III, the roles are reversed, and, as the couple progress, this time south from France, through Italy, to Africa, Michel continues to gain in strength and independence ("je suis devenu fort, à présent"—p. 160), while the health and physical and moral strength of Marceline deteriorates with ever-increasing rapidity. The mood of exhilaration is here replaced by a mood of acute disillusionment—a transition which is represented in the symbolic phrase: "A l'oasis je préfère à présent le désert." (p. 179). From the first part to the third part, Michel's ascending curve is paralleled exactly by Marceline's descending curve—a pattern which is clearly brought out by the narrator's statement: "de même que de semaine en semaine, lors de notre premier voyage, je marchais vers la guérison, de semaine en semaine, à mesure que nous avancions vers le Sud, l'état de Marceline empirait."[1]

The two curves intersect in the second part of the book, which has been described as a kind of *palier* or *lieu de repos* between parts one and

---

[1] *L'Immoraliste*, p. 170.

three. Here, it is true, the two destinies in conflict momentarily follow a parallel course, achieving a precarious balance as their hopes centre around the property of La Morinière and the baby which Marceline is expecting. But the structure of this second part reveals the same tendency towards symmetry and formalism which characterises the work as a whole. There is, here again, a clear division into three sections—a first and a final section, taking place at La Morinière, joined by a middle section, of which the background is Paris. Once more, the first of these sections could be described as positive, and represented graphically by an "ascending" curve, the third as negative and following a "descending" curve. The middle section is the section of "disturbance" which is responsible for this change of direction. Section I offers a calm picture of rustic happiness and harmony, in which we see the couple's eager anticipation of the happy event balanced by a concern for an orderly exploitation of property and a strong sense of possession. The events of the second section—the artificiality of social life in Paris, the decisive meeting with Ménalque, and finally, Marceline's miscarriage—all combine to make the second stay at La Morinière, related in the final section, a kind of negative image of the first. Echoes from one section to the other, like Michel's changed attitude to Charles, are cleverly used to underline the fact that the atmosphere is different, that harmony has been replaced by anarchy, ordered intelligence by primitive instinct, and the joy of possession by a perverse delight in "dispossession. As elsewhere in the work, these patterns of parallelism and contrast have been developed with all the rigour and logic of a geometrical formula.

In the carefully planned symmetry of the structure, certain recurring incidents take on a symbolic value and are used by the author to heighten the dramatic tension or to create an effect of irony. We have seen, in the section on irony, how certain events occurring in Part I recur in Part III, creating an impression of déjà vu with ironic overtones. In this category we can also place the coach ride from Sousse, during which Michel, fatigued by the constant jolting and his developing illness, coughs up quantities of blood into his handkerchief. This is paralleled, and re-echoed, in the coach ride of the final part, when Marceline, afflicted in turn by the same malady, also develops a persistent cough, which leads to a similar result. The irony is apparent in Marceline's sad remark, as Michel brutally tears the handkerchief from her hands, to examine it by the light of the coach: "Non, pas encore." (p. 160). Certain other events assume a symbolic significance in the light of later occurrences in the story, and represent a kind of dramatic foreshadowing of future events. Thus Michel's perverted urge to dispossess himself, towards the end of the second part, by poaching on his own property, is already foreshadowed early in the story by the episode of Moktir and the stealing of the scissors, during which Michel's reactions, as he observes himself being robbed, are exactly the same as in the later incident: a wild pounding of the heart and a violent feeling of joy.[1] Another recurring event, woven into the fabric of the structure, reappears in each of the three parts with all the insistence of a leit-motif, providing a symbolic image of Michel's rejection of God in favour of man. At each of the great moments of crisis—Michel's illness in Part I, Marceline's miscarriage in Part II, Marceline's collapse in Part III—the solace of religion is offered to the sufferer, but in each case provokes a hostile reaction, either on the part of Michel or of his wife. Michel refuses to accept it, in Part I, walks angrily out of the room in Part II, and eventually encounters the silent opposition of Marceline herself in the final scene. The symbolic rosary, so sought after by Marceline in her first illness, is rejected by her at the end—a clear symbol of the final triumph in the book of the forces of evil.[2]

Gide is not averse to employing, in *La Porte étroite* as well as in *L'Immoraliste*, a symbolic device as old as literature itself—the use of the anticipatory vision, premonition or dream, which provides a kind of dramatic foreboding of tragic events to come. Thus Michel, on the night before his departure from Biskra, has a sudden hallucinatory vision of the tragic destiny which is in store for him, "le sentiment tragique de ma vie, si violent, douloureux presque, et si impétueux que j'en aurais crié."[3] In his desire to fix forever the memory of that moment, he opens at random a book nearby, which turns out to be the Bible, and Christ's words to Peter appear before his eyes: "Maintenant tu te ceins toi-même et tu vas où tu veux aller; mais quand tu seras vieux, tu étendras les mains..." In a magnificently written passage, the author creates a dramatic premonition of the tragedy to come, anticipates symbolically the final impotence and helplessness of the hero, and, at the same time, offers an implicit judgment or criticism of the validity of his quest. This episode is paralleled,

[1] cf. *L'Immoraliste* p. 50 and p. 143.

[2] Gide's intentions become clear as the result of his addition of the rosary incident to the final scene. This did not appear in the first MS. of the book.

[3] *L'Immoraliste* p. 55.

in *La Porte étroite*, by the dream of Alissa.[1] The technique here is almost identical. Alissa tells Jérôme of a strange dream which has haunted her since the previous night. In the dream she saw Jérôme as dead, while she herself remained alive—a situation so intolerable for her that death was eventually replaced by absence. But their separation proved so difficult to end that Alissa, as she slept, had the vivid impression that they were to remain apart for a long, long time—indeed, for the rest of their lives. Gide's intention is obvious. The dream clearly serves as a dramatic preparation for tragic events, a symbolic foreshadowing of a heroic, but futile quest for virtue.

To turn from the structure of *L'Immoraliste* to that of *La Porte étroite*, is to have the illusion of moving from a world of formalism and symmetry to a world of diversity and complexity. True, *La Porte étroite* has been no less rigorously composed than *L'Immoraliste*, and symbolic patterns have been used with similar effect, but symmetry is here concealed beneath the considerable subtlety and variety of the texture. The result is a structure appearing to grow naturally out of the situation in question, rather than one too obviously guided by the hand of the author. Consider the subtle variations in technique with which the happenings of the story are presented. Even in the first half of the book, which consists uniformly of Jérôme's narrative of the events, the range extends from apparently disjointed *souvenirs* at the beginning to a highly dramatic version of an episode in chapter four. Then, from chapter five onwards, the technique becomes progressively more complex, with the skilful use of letters and diary to supplement Jérôme's narrative. From that moment on, no one chapter resembles another: Alissa's letters are woven into the fabric of the *récit* with continually varying effect, and extracts from her diary are presented to the reader in the form of an entirely separate but very revealing document.

A brief analysis of the structure of chapters one and four should serve to indicate the variety of Gide's art in *La Porte étroite*. Jérôme begins his story in the most discursive manner possible, apologizing for the lack of polish in his presentation of the events ("ils sont en lambeaux par endroits"), but refusing to deck them out in the garb of art. And so he goes on from one recollection to another, apparently without order or coherence, speaking briefly of his cousins, then turning to Aunt Lucile, returning once more to his cousins with a more detailed portrait, and

[1] *La Porte étroite* p. 48.

finally coming back to the events concerning Lucile. At times his memory appears to falter, as he has trouble fixing the exact dates of events occurring as far back as twenty years previously. At one point, after a longish description of early childhood memories attached to the property at Fongueusemare, he appears to check himself and promises to confine himself to the events relevant to the story (p. 11). He makes little attempt to fuse the outlines of the story into a smooth-flowing narrative —the "joints" of the structure continually show through, as when he indicates, for example, that "avant de parler du triste événement qui bouleversa notre famille, ... il est temps que je vous parle de ma cousine." (p. 19), or when, after having done this, he clumsily reverts to the episode concerning his aunt: "je veux d'abord et pour ne plus ensuite reparler d'elle, achever de vous raconter ce qui a trait à ma tante." (p. 20) We must not be deluded. In spite of Jérôme's rambling, digressive manner and the apparent artlessness of the narrative (which constitute a deliberate attempt by Gide to convey the character of the narrator), by the end of the chapter we have been given all the essentials of the situation, with hardly a detail which has not been carefully chosen for the immediate needs of the story. As an exposition, it is a cleverly disguised *tour de force*.

Chapter four displays a technique which is the very antithesis of the art of Chapter one. To relate the important episode in which Jérôme learns for the first time of Juliette's love for him, the narrator adopts a highly dramatic technique, which, while hardly appropriate to the character of Jérôme as we have come to know him, nevertheless gives relief to a *récit* which had been up to then a little lacking in colour. Jérôme narrates the episode, not with the omniscience conferred by events which have already taken place, but with all the astonishment and bewilderment of an observer involved in the happenings for the first time. The rhythm of the scene is governed by a series of dramatic departures and returns on the part of Jérôme—a pattern symbolic of his weak, indecisive nature, of his constant failure to face up to reality. In each case, the strain of suspense becomes too much for him, and he escapes from the warm interior of Aunt Plantier's house, gaily bedecked for the Christmas festivities, to the cold, sobering air of the streets, wharves or cliffs of Le Havre. On his return, on each occasion some dramatic event has occurred in the house, but nothing is explained to us, we see the people and incidents through Jérôme's non-comprehending eyes, we experience the same puzzlement and suspense as himself, until finally Abel drags him off to reveal to him—and to us—the key to the mystery.

The style itself, with its dramatic terseness and brevity, also plays its part in establishing the atmosphere of rising tension. The final scene, with its melodramatically conceived *tableau*, provides a rather obviously contrived climax to the chapter, but one totally in harmony with the dramatic spirit of the whole episode.

This chapter is quite unique in the book. Thereafter, the technique of *récit*, interspersed with the quotation of letters and diary, becomes extraordinarily subtle and complex. Its basic effect is to achieve an illusion of greater authenticity and realism, for what more natural way is there of revealing Alissa's successive states of mind than to quote her own letters or private diary? How, otherwise, could the narrator be expected to know her most secret and intimate thoughts, unless verisimilitude is to be sacrificed? As we penetrate more deeply into the complex fabric of *récit*, letters and diary, the subtlety of Gide's art becomes more and more apparent, and it becomes manifestly impossible, within the scope of this brief essay, to indicate more than a few of the many forms which it takes. We have already considered, in the section on irony, the technique by which illuminating flashes of light are made to pass from diary to *récit*, enabling the reader to distinguish true motives from false or pointing up ironically the tragic non-comprehension of the narrator. In these cases, one version *contradicts* the other. But this is only one of the many uses of the technique. Sometimes letters may almost take the place of *récit*, and be used simply to tell the story, as in Chapter five, where Alissa's letters are strung together with a minimum of commentary by Jérôme. This device not only advances the story, but allows the reader a penetrating glimpse into the inner workings of Alissa's mind. At other times, the same motif or incident may recur in different versions, setting up echoes between two points of the book and creating a third-dimensional effect, an illusion of greater depth. As examples, the bundle of letters from Jérôme which Alissa comes to re-read in the garden, and the amethyst cross which, at the end, she wants to give him as a souvenir—incidents which are evoked in Jérôme's narrative and re-echoed, poignantly, in Alissa's diary. Similarly, Alissa's feelings of melancholy and *dépaysement* during her stay at Aigues-Vives with Juliette—first described in a letter to Jérôme (p. 119), then re-echoed in an entry in her diary (p. 177).

More significantly, a second version of an incident may be used to *complement* a first, to throw a fuller light on events of which only the barest outlines have been given the first time. In particular, this serves to lay bare motives beneath actions, to provide a psychological commentary running parallel to the events. Letter may illuminate *récit*, like the letter from Alissa quoted by Jérôme immediately after the disastrous *promenade* at Orcher (p. 130). Or diary may complement narrative, as with Jérôme's account of the final reunion with Alissa at Fongueusemare, in which he had foolishly placed so much hope. It is only when we turn to the Diary (pp. 186-7) for Alissa's analysis of her state of mind at the time of this reunion, that we can fully understand the astonishing: "Nous ne sommes pas nés pour le bonheur" which, at one stroke, reduced Jérôme to the depths of despair. Finally, Alissa's diary may illuminate her own letters, disclosing to the reader the hidden reasons for actions which she dare not confess in her letters to Jérôme. In this way the Diary probes even deeper into her secret motives, laying bare the very depths of her soul. If one of her letters to Jérôme poses the question as to why Juliette's happiness succeeded merely in filling her, Alissa, with melancholy (p. 119), it is only in her Diary that she admits honestly to herself the true reason for this: "Pourquoi me mentirais-je à moi-même? ... Ce bonheur que j'ai tant souhaité, jusqu'à offrir de lui sacrifier mon bonheur, je souffre de le voir obtenu sans peine, et différent de ce qu'elle et moi nous imaginions qu'il dût être."[1]

Similar flashes of light constantly illumine the whole texture of *La Porte étroite*, and these are but a few examples of its subtle, suggestive power, which becomes more apparent with each successive reading. In this book, unlike *L'Immoraliste*, there are no simplified or over-obvious formal patterns imposed on the events, yet such symmetry does exist, even though for the most part concealed by the greater complexity of the novelist's art. This symmetry is rather more obvious in the parallelism of certain episodes, like the two "eavesdropping" scenes in the garden at Fongueusemare (pp. 32-37 and pp. 51-55), or in the alternating rhythm of separation and reunion (in this same garden), which marks the evolution of the love-story and forms the main fabric of the plot.

Of more subtle effect is the symbolism of *les portes*, which constantly reappears in the book under various guises, taking on all the force and evocative power of a recurring *leitmotif*. With the images of "doors" are associated images of "roads" or "paths" and both gain considerably in depth from an association with real objects in the text. We see the device first used in the biblical text chosen by Pastor Vautier to illustrate his

[1] *La Porte étroite* p. 179.

sermon. Here the *porte large* and the *chemin spacieux* become symbols of the path of pleasure, lust and self-indulgence followed by Lucile Bucolin, while the *porte étroite* and the *voie resserrée* are used to illustrate the way to virtue and godliness. These symbolic *portes* are then identified with real *portes* by Jérôme as he daydreams in the church—the *porte large* becomes the door to his Aunt Lucile's room, significantly open in the preceding scene, and bathed in light, while the *porte étroite* becomes, in his dream, identified with the door to Alissa's room, in contrast closed and enveloped in semi-darkness.

In that scene, the same image is also used to illustrate Jérôme's particular conception of "virtue"—one in which he moves towards his ideal hand in hand with Alissa (p. 28). This is further developed in Jérôme's subsequent recall of the image, when, after the receipt of Alissa's letter (p. 144), he finds himself ensnared in *le piège de la vertu*. *Le sentier étroit* now becomes also *un sentier montant et ardu* and, for him, "le terrain ne se rétrécirait jamais trop vite, pour ne supporter plus que nous deux". But, as the tragic events develop, the image takes on a quite contrasting colour, becoming now the embodiment of Alissa's totally different conception of virtue: "Mais non! la route que vous nous enseignez, Seigneur, est une route étroite—étroite à n'y pouvoir marcher deux de front."[1] What was before, for Jérôme, a glorious symbol of renunciation, now becomes a symbol representing the personal tragedy of Alissa—an effect which is reinforced by the association, at the end of the story, with another real *porte—la porte du potager*. In this scene, where Jérôme lies sobbing bitterly against the locked and bolted garden gate, behind which Alissa has retired for the last time, the symbol of the *portes* takes on its most poignant development. For here *la porte étroite* becomes *la porte fermée*—a symbol of the irrevocable triumph of Alissa's point of view. Henceforth, in spite of Alissa's repentant return, later that same night, to re-open the little *porte à secret* (p. 197), the door will remain forever closed between Jérôme and Alissa.

(b) *Characters*

Gide, even in his more complex works of fiction, like *Les Caves du Vatican* and *Les Faux-Monnayeurs*, is no creator of memorable and fully rounded living characters. This is still more apparent in works of narrower dimensions, such as the *récits*. In *L'Immoraliste*, in particular,

---

[1] *La Porte étroite* p. 188.

the minor characters exist purely in terms of their functional purpose, which is to serve as stimuli for setting in motion the psychological reactions of Michel. They have little more than a symbolic value, reflecting the successive states of mind of the hero, and, as they take their place in the ever changing but symmetrical patterns of the work, they become themselves an integral part of these patterns. One is tempted to say of Ménalque, Charles, even of Marceline herself, what E. M. Forster said of Henry James' *The Ambassadors*: "This drastic curtailment, both of the number of human beings and of their attributes, is in the interests of the pattern . . . A pattern must emerge, and anything that emerged from the pattern must be pruned off as wanton distraction. Who so wanton as human beings?"[1] It is indeed the particular attributes of human beings that are to be found wanting in the secondary characters of *L'Immoraliste*.[2] Existing primarily as cogs in a wheel, they hardly exist in their own right, and remain simplifications, even abstractions.

Charles, the eldest son of Bocage, is brought into the story to serve as the embodiment of Michel's newly-awakened appreciation of life and the senses, while this is still in its positive and constructive phase. As in the case of the native boy, Bachir, it is above all the healthiness and handsomeness of Charles that is stressed ("C'était un beau gaillard, riche de santé, souple, bien fait" (p. 85)). Charles, like Bachir, symbolises three distinct aspects of Michel's mental attitude: first, an obsession with good health natural in a man who has just recovered from a serious illness; secondly, a new awareness of the body and of physical beauty, the product of a sudden re-awakening to life, and finally, the first sub-conscious glimmerings of homosexual feelings, to be more clearly indicated in the closing pages of the book. In Charles the *positive* side of Michel's transformation is stressed, and this is borne out in the happy atmosphere of the actions performed in common, in the early morning journeys together on horseback through the property of La Morinière, from which Michel would return "ivre d'air, étourdi de vitesse, . . . l'esprit plein de santé, d'appétit, de fraîcheur."[3] But when *la courbe descendante* of the story begins, when good is gradually transformed into evil and positive values into negative, at that moment

---

[1] *Aspects of the Novel*, p. 206.

[2] Bocage, with his fussiness and self-righteous complacency, is perhaps an exception.

[3] *L'Immoraliste* pp. 94-5.

Charles is superseded by Bute and by Bocage's second son, Alcide, who becomes a figure as clearly symbolic as that of his brother. Good looks, cleanness and grace are replaced by "un méchant galopin, à l'œil vert, aux cheveux filasse, à l'expression chafouine",[1] and the invigorating rides through the fresh morning dew are replaced by night prowlings with Alcide in search of illegal game, whence Michel will return "ivre de nuit, de vie sauvage et d'anarchie, trempé, boueux."[2] Characters like Charles and Alcide, it will be seen, have little more existence than pawns in a chess game visibly manipulated by the hands of the author. They simply represent successive phases in the development of the hero's state of mind.

This same tendency towards simplification and symmetry is visible in Gide's original intention to create a third member of Bocage's family —a daughter, who was to be called Berthe and who would counterbalance the two sons, Charles and Alcide. Already, to indicate the contrast between the attitudes of Michel and Marceline, and to reveal Marceline's strong maternal instincts, the author had portrayed her preference for ailing, puny and deformed native children (cf. pp. 42 and 50). The introduction of Berthe, "la pauvre enfant bossue", was obviously intended to accentuate this trait: Marceline was to take this daughter under her wing, guide her, train her, educate her, bestow on her the full warmth of her maternal affection. The first manuscript of *L'Immoraliste* shows the contrast between the resplendent health and good looks of Charles and the pitiful deformity of Berthe: "Elle était infirme; je ne sais quelle sournoise maladie l'avait douloureusement décolorée, courbée, avait enlevé à ses membres la force, sans apporter la grâce en échange."[3] In the final text, however, Gide abandoned the idea of introducing this character—fortunately, perhaps, because Berthe would simply have become one more symbolic figure, one further motif in the intricate patterns of similarity and contrast which make up the fabric of *L'Immoraliste*.

The character of Ménalque is no less of an abstraction. For once, Gide appears to have departed from his firm artistic principle of representing ideas by action and events, not by direct preaching. For Ménalque is nothing but a mouthpiece for the ideas which are to insinuate themselves gradually into Michel's mind. He, too, represents a

---

[1] *Ibid.*, p. 143.   [2] *Ibid.*, p. 146.
[3] First MS. of *L'Immoraliste*, in the Bibliothèque Doucet.

phase in the development of Michel's mental attitude, appearing suddenly, just at the right moment, in the middle of the book, without prior
motivation or warning, and disappearing just as suddenly, once his
mission as converter is accomplished. Gide, in reducing the character to
bare essentials, in limiting Ménalque to his symbolic role as a promoter
of ideas, has at the same time deprived him of any semblance of real life.
It was important that Ménalque should represent the ideal embodiment
of certain principles of individualism, and thus all human failings and
weaknesses in the character have been rigorously suppressed; witness the
suppression of this passage from the first manuscript, in which Ménalque,
remarking on his coming departure from Paris, for once betrays some
warmth of human feeling:—"Il se tut un instant, puis ajouta—mais si
j'avais femme et enfant, ah! partirais-je? Sans doute je resterais."[1]
Unfortunately, such perfection, such singleness of purpose exist only
in an ideal world, and Ménalque, as a consequence, fails completely to
come to life. Even Marceline, that frail and pathetic creature, is sacrificed
to the essentially dramatic conception of the *récit*. To such an extent
is the light focussed on Michel, and Michel alone, that she remains
beside him but a pale shadowy figure, without the depth or substance
of real life, and existing primarily for the reactions she provokes in the
mind of the hero.

La Porte étroite, because of the greater complexity of the story and
what Gide referred to as "the invention of the double plot", has a
larger array of secondary characters than *L'Immoraliste*. Patterns of
similarity and contrast emerge, here also, from the relations between
the various characters. At the beginning of the story, two contrasting
characters make a brief appearance, only to disappear completely thereafter, but leaving a profound imprint on the hero and heroine. These are
Jérôme's mother, whose puritanical influence is largely responsible for
his obsession with virtue and his sexual inhibitions, and the mother of
Alissa, whose looseness of morals provokes a similar puritanical reaction
in the mind of her daughter. In the second chapter, in a significant
conversation between Alissa's father and the two cousins, the resemblances between the younger members of the family and the older
generation are clearly brought out: "Nous n'étions pas bien différents,
je vous assure, de ce que vous paraissez aujourd'hui. J'étais assez pareil à

---

[1] This last sentence has been deleted from the MS. in the Bibliothèque
Doucet.

toi, Jérôme; plus peut-être que je ne le sais. Félicie ressemblait beaucoup à ce qu'est à présent Juliette ... Oui, physiquement même." And Miss Ashburton, turning around to Jérôme, remarks: "Ta mère, c'est Alissa qui la rappelle."[1]

These remarks, together with other hints, give us the key to Gide's construction of the characters in *La Porte étroite*. Of the six principal figures who appear in the remainder of the book, three clearly belong to one group, whom we may call the "introverts", characterised by their seriousness, their pre-disposition to melancholy and their contemplative natures. These include Jérôme, Alissa and her father. On the other hand, there are the "extroverts", those pre-disposed to gaiety, exuberance and effusiveness, and whose charm, like Juliette's beauty, "semblait extérieure et se livrer à tous d'un seul coup."[2] In this group are to be placed Abel, Juliette and Tante Plantier. The secret of Gide's art in character construction lies here in the skilful balancing of light against dark, in achieving relief by placing the members of one group in contrasting relationship with the members of the other. Juliette is used as a foil to Alissa, Abel as a foil to Jérôme, and Tante Plantier, with her gushing effusiveness, provides an effective contrast to the deep seriousness of both Alissa and Jérôme. In this way, variety and colour are given to the *récit*, and a monotonous uniformity of tone is successfully avoided.

One cannot help being struck by the vividness with which the secondary characters are portrayed in *La Porte étroite*—in particular, realistic gestures and life-like dialogue give a sharpness of outline to such picturesque characters as Lucile Bucolin, Abel Vautier and Aunt Félicie Plantier. Little details like Lucile moistening her finger with saliva to wet the corners of her eyes, Tante Plantier's sudden sob as she refers to Jérôme's late mother, Abel's joyful rolling in the cushions of the coach bringing Jérôme and him to Paris—all this has the authentic ring of real life and marks a clear advance over the technique of character portrayal used in *L'Immoraliste*. The patterns of symmetry and contrast are still there, but are well concealed beneath a skilful attempt at realistic characterisation.

These characters, however, are but the accessories to the drama. The true measure of Gide's success must ultimately depend on his treatment of the chief protagonists[3] of the two *récits*. And, to judge this,

[1] *La Porte étroite* pp. 46-7.

[2] *La Porte étroite*, p. 20.

[3] i.e. in *La Porte étroite*—Alissa. Jérôme remains a passive, neutral

we must adopt different criteria from those which we usually apply to the criticism of characters in a novel. Let us not, then, expect, as in Balzac or Dickens, the creation of powerfully drawn and fully rounded characters, which as a result of their intensely living qualities, reach out from the particular to the universal and become "types". Gide does not belong to that class of novelists whose methods are founded primarily on a close observation of life around them—the novelist who, as he put it, "voit d'abord le geste d'autrui, l'événement, et . . . l'explique et l'interprète."[1] Gide's basic starting point is from within himself—a feeling, emotion or idea which takes hold of his mind and seeks expression in the work of art, so that the author "invente événements et personnages les mieux propres à mettre ces émotions en valeur."[1] The physical appearance of his heroes thus becomes irrelevant, for it is the original idea or emotion which counts, and even the addition to the character of other psychological traits can be considered an unnecessary complication of the issue. The result is a reduction to essentials and an idealisation or stylisation of the main characters of the *récit*. They each represent an idea—even an *idée fixe*, which so dominates their nature that they leave the bounds of everyday life and enter a rarefied world of their own. Michel and Alissa have very little link with the general run of humanity, with the external world so faithfully, if laboriously, constructed by the *romanciers naturalistes*.

They have a closer link with the world of the theatre, especially tragedy. We think of each of them not so much as a physical presence, but as a mind in the throes of a violent conflict. Like the great figures of tragedy, Phèdre for example, their lives are dominated by a single obsession, which, coming into conflict with natural human emotions, gradually poisons their minds and brings about their eventual downfall. And it is precisely through the dramatic portrayal of a mind in conflict that these characters, in other respects so removed from normal life, re-enter the living world of human beings. Gide once again demonstrates his capacity to breathe life into situations closely related with his own experience, to re-create conflicts in his heroes which are but the projection of his own inner *angoisse*. As a result, the portrayal of the inner

character, corresponding to Marceline in *L'Immoraliste*. He is there almost solely for the reactions he provokes in the mind of Alissa, and it is on the conflict in Alissa's mind that the full light of the drama is focussed.

[1] *Un Esprit non prévenu*, in *Divers* (NRF, 1931), p. 61.

struggle in Michel and in Alissa takes on an intensity which is deeply moving. The conflict, in Michel, between the "old man" and the new, between the quest for individualism and love for Marceline, leads to anguished self-questionings and vacillations which carry all the conviction of a real-life struggle. The case of Alissa is even more poignant, as she struggles to assume, before Jérôme, a mask of impassive indifference, while, within, her mind is torn by a cruel conflict between her ideal and her overwhelming love for her cousin. Alissa's diary, as the tragic record of a human heart at variance with itself, represents, indeed, a living document almost without parallel in the history of modern French literature.

These characters, then, though idealised, remain true. Their inner contradictions, their inconsistencies, and their repressions, are those of real human beings, and bestow on Michel and Alissa a psychological truth which richly compensates for their lack of physical presence.

(c) *Background*

We have seen Gide's lack of interest in descriptions for their own sake. His descriptions of people or landscapes, usually brief, are always there for a set purpose and remain indissolubly connected with the artistic design of the work as a whole. Thus, in *L'Immoraliste* and *La Porte étroite*, the brief evocations of background, landscape or climate play their part in the general symbolism of the structure. They, too, have their patterns and recurring *leitmotifs* which generally follow the changing moods of the story. This device is not new. Ever since Rousseau and the Romantics, landscapes have been mirrors reflecting the emotions of those observing them, and Nature has been seen as sympathetic or as hostile to the poet. Symbolism further developed the mysterious *correspondances* between Nature and the mind of the poet, and the evocation of a landscape became the evocation of a state of mind. Attracted by the Symbolist theories at the beginning of his career, Gide displayed a fondness for symbolic landscapes in much of his early work, like *Le Traité du Narcisse*, *Le Voyage d'Urien* (really a series of imaginary landscapes reflecting varying moods) and *La Tentative amoureuse*, where the narrator's purpose is to "raconter un rapport de saisons avec l'âme".[1] In an early preface, Gide even developed a theory of the relationship between landscape and emotion, claiming their complete interdepend-

---

[1] *La Tentative amoureuse*, p. 82. (*Romans*, Pléiade edition).

ence and "reversibility": "Il y a là une sorte d'algèbre esthétique; émotion et manifeste forment équation; l'un est l'équivalent de l'autre. Qui dit *émotion* dira donc *paysage*; et qui dit *paysage* devra donc connaître *émotion*."[1]

It is in this spirit that we are to interpret Gide's use of background in *L'Immoraliste* and *La Porte étroite*. The Symbolist theories are long forgotten, but their effect still lingers on in the symbolic evocations of landscape to be found in both *récits*. Background here serves as a dramatic or poetic accompaniment to the events of the story, continually changing to reflect its varying moods and heightening and intensifying these moods. "Pas le paysage lui-même; l'émotion par lui causée." (*André Walter*). Thus, during Michel's first journey, the bursting luxuriance of the African spring, the pleasant greenery of the oasis, the pure air and radiant sunshine of Italy, provide a harmonious accompaniment to the physical and spiritual regeneration of the hero. During the stay at La Morinière, the copious harvests, the abundant crops of apples, "ces vaches pleines dans ces opulentes prairies" (p. 83), in short, "l'éclatement fécond de la libre nature" (p. 84), offers a faithful image of the harmony and balance of this happy period, when, in fact, Marceline herself is pregnant with Michel's child. But when happiness has turned to disillusionment, in the final journey to Africa, then the Italian skies cloud over, the sun gives way to bitter wind and dreary rain, and the inviting shade and fertility of the oasis changed to the barrenness of the desert, seared by *le simoun ardent* or *le sirocco aride*.

The use of this device is even more striking in *La Porte étroite*, where the garden at Fongueusemare, the scene of more than one reconciliation between the estranged lovers, is used as a symbolic décor to reflect the happy mood of these reunions. At such times, the whole garden is ablaze with sunshine and perfumed by a profusion of flowers. At such times, all misunderstandings and resentment seem to vanish in the radiance of nature around them. One can find no better example of this concurrence of mood and natural setting than in the episode describing the joyful period of their love. Here surroundings, weather and emotions merge into a happy and harmonious union, offering a striking illustration of this "reversibility" of landscape and feeling that had so preoccupied the young Gide: "L'été, cette année, fut splendide. Tout semblait pénétré d'azur. Notre ferveur triomphait du mal, de la mort; l'ombre

---

[1] *Romans* (Pléiade edition), p. 1464.

reculait devant nous. Chaque matin j'étais éveillé par ma joie; je me levais dès l'aurore, à la rencontre du jour m'élançais . . . Quand je rêve à ce temps, je le revois plein de rosée."[1] Full of lyrical effect in this case, the device is used, finally, for dramatic purposes in the sombre narration of Jérôme's and Alissa's last meeting. Filled with resentment against virtue, Jérôme scarcely replies to Alissa's questions. The mood is tense and anguished, when suddenly the setting sun breaks out from behind the clouds, "envahissant d'un luxe frémissant les champs vides et comblant d'une profusion subite l'étroit vallon qui s'ouvrait à nos pieds."[2] Almost at once, the vision has disappeared, the sun has gone from view, but the warmth of its radiance, for one brief moment, fills Jérôme with a kind of "extase dorée où mon ressentiment s'évaporait et je n'entendais plus en moi que l'amour." This apocalyptic vision of happiness, this nostalgic and fleeting glimpse of a love which might have been, takes on, from the dramatic contrast with the surrounding events, a tragic poignancy. Symbolism forms here an integral part of the dramatic structure of the *récit*.

From all that has been said here, and in the rest of this chapter, it follows that once we accept *L'Immoraliste* and *La Porte étroite* in the spirit in which they have been composed, any criticism of their artificiality is beside the point. Artificial they are, and stylised, but the symbolism inherent in their structure is a part of the author's total conception, which is that of a poet, rather than that of a novelist. These *récits* have, indeed, as Professor Brée says, been composed with all the rigour and logic of a poem, and their subtle, suggestive power, their indefinable power of emotion, has real affinities with the world of poetry.

CHAPTER FOUR

Affinities

André Gide is a writer whose thought reaches out beyond the confines of his own work to rejoin the intellectual aspirations of other thinkers of his time. His mind is, however, sufficiently complex and many-sided

---

[1] *La Porte étroite*, p. 47.   [2] *Ibid.*, p. 165.

to be able to embrace a variety of attitudes without necessarily under-
going the direct influence of others. Rather than influence, one may
speak of an indirect assimilation of the mood of the age, arising from
an acute sensitivity to current trends and tendencies. In this category
can be placed analogies which we find between aspects of his thought
and the thought of Nietzsche and Freud. At the same time, Gide's
thought is in many ways prophetic. As regards both ideas and techniques,
his work offers a remarkable anticipation of tendencies occurring in
more recent periods of French literature. He is at once a spokesman
for his own age and a herald of the future.

From this point of view, *L'Immoraliste* is both the product of a certain
intellectual climate at the end of the 19th century and the anticipation
of a state of mind which is to dominate French literature towards the
middle of the present century. Michel's attempt at full self-realisation
has obvious links with Nietzsche's cult of the superman, which found
favour with many French intellectuals about 1900. The question of
an influence of Nietzsche on Gide has been sufficiently discussed for us
to be able to deny its existence and to re-affirm Gide's own statement
that the basis of his thought would have remained essentially the same
even if Nietzsche had never lived. Yet the similarity of climate is
undeniable. *L'Immoraliste* takes its place among works expressing the
conflict, at the end of the 19th century, between the individual and
society—a phenomenon which has been acutely analysed by Micheline
Tison-Braun in her book *La Crise de l'humanisme*, and of which the
philosophy of Nietzsche remains one important manifestation, or
symptom. Michel's (and Ménalque's) revolt against society, their
assertion of the supremacy of the individual, become part of a whole
movement of ideas current at that time. Mme Tison-Braun has well
defined a theme which is to become of vital importance in the whole
of Gide's subsequent work: "La pression sociale substitue à un être
humain authentique une fiction conforme aux vérités acceptées, et . . . il
faut dénoncer ce pharisaïsme afin de retrouver la vérité individuelle sous
la fiction sociale."[1] It is this problem which is at the very heart of
Michel's dilemma.

At the same time, *L'Immoraliste*, by its moral and social implications,
looks forward to the age of Existentialism. Everett Knight, in his
interesting book, *Literature considered as Philosophy*, has traced the links

[1] *op. cit.*, p. 372.

between Gide's thought and modern Existentialism. Gide would have been the first to be astonished by such an attempt, and Knight perhaps goes too far in his efforts to make Gide into *un existentialiste sans le savoir*. Nevertheless, there is some validity in his claims. The denial of absolute principles and values, the condemnation of bourgeois conformism, the attempt to realise one's potentialities by individual action and self-development, the knowledge that "the only Self we will ever have is one which *we ourselves create*"[1]—all this is an essential part of the doctrine of Sartre and at the same time cannot fail to evoke in our minds Michel's own protest and action. Camus' portrayal, in *L'Etranger*, of an absurd world, Meursault's revolt against it by the cultivation of the instincts and the denial of reason, the same author's portrait of another social rebel in Caligula, who, as Professor Brée points out, "cherche, lui aussi, jusqu'où peut aller la liberté d'enfreindre les lois humaines"[2]—all this, too, inevitably reminds us of Gide's Michel, who thus becomes an authentic precursor of the fictional heroes of Albert Camus.

If *L'Immoraliste* remains an important work because it is in the very centre of the current which leads to a significant part of contemporary French thought, one could claim no such importance for *La Porte étroite*. Even Gide himself, when writing this book in 1907, found it "en anachronisme avec ce que nous pensons, sentons et voulons aujourd'hui."[3] And yet Elizabeth Fraser, in her thesis *Le Renouveau religieux d'après le roman français de 1886 à 1914*, puts forward a convincing case to show mystical and spiritual aspirations similar to Alissa's in a number of other French novels of that period. The truth is that the French literary *durée* is, at any given moment, sufficiently complex to embrace the most widely differing attitudes, just as Gide's mind is sufficiently Protean to permit of identification with more than one current of thought. The real Gide, however, is to be found in the sum total of these conflicting tendencies, not in any one taken separately.

It might have been appropriate to point this out to Albert Guerard, who has attached such overwhelming importance to the Freudian implications of Gide's work. But, to deny absolutely these implications, as does Everett Knight,[4] would appear equally to sin by excess. Gide's

[1] Knight, *op. cit.*, p. 112.   [2] *André Gide*, p. 175.
[3] *Journal* (1907) (Pléiade edition) p. 255.
[4] *op. cit.*, pp. 92-3. Knight finds the Freudian theory of man as a helpless victim of the subconscious to be incompatible with the alleged pre-

whole early life is itself a striking illustration of Freudian principles, as Jean Delay has shown in his admirable book *La Jeunesse d'André Gide*. But, more significantly, from our point of view, Gide seems to have had Freudian insights some time before the work of Freud achieved its great celebrity in the 1920's, and to have applied certain of these principles in his early literary work. In 1922, he wrote in his *Journal*: "Freud. Le freudisme ... Depuis dix ans, quinze ans, j'en fais sans le savoir."[2] And it is precisely his remarkable anticipation of Freudian principles in both *L'Immoraliste* and *La Porte étroite* which adds much to their originality and makes them into up-to-date versions of the old *roman d'analyse*.

We have already studied, in a previous section, the part played by the sub-conscious in the actions of Michel, Jérôme and Alissa, seen especially in their need to justify their acts by a form of unconscious rationalisation. But there is also evidence to suggest that the main-springs of the action in both *récits* are to be found at least partly in motives which we recognise today as Freudian. Michel's assertion of his individualism is, at the conscious level, an attempt to discover his true personality, but, at a deeper level, submerged in Michel's subconscious, it becomes partly a compensation for certain weaknesses in his psychological make-up. This particularly concerns the complex nature of his marital relationship with Marceline. The first manuscript of *L'Immoraliste*, already referred to, includes a passage showing the violence of his physical desire for his wife, which immediately disappears as soon as he comes into her presence. The one occasion when Michel achieves a satisfactory consummation of his marriage (after his fight with the coachman), is followed by the most complete reaction in his attitude to Marceline. The cult of individualism is temporarily forgotten, and Marceline is given all the loving care and attention which up to then she had lacked. The first manuscript of *L'Immoraliste* is even more explicit in this regard than the final text: here the influence exerted upon Michel by his wife after their one night of love is shown to reach a quite extraordinary degree, while his new interest in the authentic self is now ignored, even despised ("mon âpre convoitise de la vie et

existentialism of Gide, which he seeks to establish. According to his view, Gide's thought foreshadowed that of the Existentialists, which is that man creates his own freedom and his own destiny by his actions.

[2] *Journal* (1922) (Pléiade edition), p. 729.

ma sauvagerie de la veille m'apparurent déplaisantes et maladives; je n'en sentais plus que l'excès.") It is also significant that the loss of the child which was the product of this one happy union and which offered Michel the badly-needed reassurance of his own virility, is followed by an even more frenzied renewal of the pursuit of individualism. Subconscious guilt about personal inadequacy and the recourse to mechanisms of compensation are both well-known to us since Freud, and the suggestion of these processes at work in the mind of Michel gives an added depth to the character, without in any way implying that Gide was here consciously guided by the principles of Freud.

A similar depth is given to the character of Alissa by the suggestion, which Gide has deliberately exploited, that her actions are motivated not only by her ideal of virtue, but also, to some extent, by subconscious guilt feelings about her mother's conduct, which lead to sexual inhibitions in the daughter. She refuses Jérôme not only because she is seeking a mystical communion with God, but also because she is afraid of life. Or rather the two go together, and in Freudian terms, the one attitude is a sublimation of the other. This is particularly apparent in the episode already analysed,[1] when Alissa's guilt complex about sex is the cause of her great mental anguish in the presence of Jérôme. If Gide was unaware of the existence of Freud when he wrote *La Porte étroite*, at least his conception of the character of Alissa, based on "la 'faute' de la mère, d'où le besoin vague d'expiation",[2] shows his remarkable anticipation of the Freudian theories. Herein lies part of the originality of *La Porte étroite*, as Professor Brée rightly pointed out: "Avoir placé dans le refoulement l'obstacle à la réalisation de l'amour et avoir montré la formation de cet obstacle chez deux enfants exaltés pour qui l'amour sensuel sera entouré d'un halo d'horreur et de remords, voilà ce que Gide a apporté de plus neuf à son roman."[3]

To study *L'Immoraliste* and *La Porte étroite*, then, is not only to enjoy dramatic stories, soberly yet vividly related by one of the great stylists of modern French literature, it is also to gain an insight into contemporary attitudes and trends of thought. Gide is not only of his own generation, he belongs to the whole of the modern age, so that even Sartre, who first asserted himself by reacting against him, admitted upon the author's death in 1951: "Toute la pensée française de ces trente

[1] cf. p. 38.   [2] Letter to Claudel (10 June 1909).
[3] *André Gide*, p. 197.

dernières années, qu'elle le voulût ou non, quelles que fussent par ailleurs ses autres coordonnées, Marx, Hegel, Kierkegaard, devait se définir *aussi* par rapport à Gide."[1] His whole work, and not only *L'Immoraliste*, represents a triumphant assertion of the rights of the individual and an unceasing, restless search for truth. A great modern humanist, afflicted with the tragic *angoisse* and uncertainty of the present age, but never losing faith in the future of man, Gide stretches beyond the barriers of time to become, with Montaigne, "notre perpétuel contemporain."

---

[1] *Les Temps modernes*, No. 55 (March 1951), p. 1538.

Select Bibliography

(1) General Studies on the Work of Gide

(a) in French:

G. Brée, André Gide—L'insaisissable Protée (Les Belles Lettres, 1953) (an excellent general survey of Gide's work).

R. Fernandez, André Gide (Corréa, 1931)
(an early, but perceptive study of Gide).

L. Pierre-Quint, André Gide (Stock, 1952)
(interesting study of "l'homme, sa vie, son oeuvre")
(b) in English:

L. A. Bisson, André Gide (1869-1951) A memorial lecture.
(Queen's University, Belfast, 1952).

A. Guerard, André Gide (Harvard University Press, 1951)
(intelligent analysis, perhaps with over-emphasis on the Freudian implications of Gide's work).

J. Hytier, André Gide (Translated by R. Howard: Doubleday N.Y., 1962)
(English translation of a justly famous study, which considers Gide's work from the aesthetic point of view).

G. W. Ireland, Gide (Oliver & Boyd, 1963)

J. O'Brien, Portrait of André Gide (Secker and Warburg, 1953).

E. Starkie, André Gide (Bowes and Bowes, 1953). (in a brief 60 pages, the best general introduction to the work of Gide.)

(2) Biography

A. Gide, Si le grain ne meurt, in Journal 1939-1949, Souvenirs. (Pléiade, N.R.F., 1954). (Gide's memoirs of his early life, revealing the sources of both L'Immoraliste and La Porte étroite.)

J. Delay, La Jeunesse d'André Gide (N.R.F., 2 vols., 1956-58). (Admirable survey of the early life and intellectual development of Gide)

R.-G. Nobécourt, Les Nourritures normandes d'André Gide (Editions Médicis, 1949) (For the origins of L'Immoraliste and La Porte étroite in Gide's early life in Normandy.)

J. Schlumberger, Madeleine et André Gide (N.R.F., 1956) (Gide's relations with his cousin and wife, helpful for an appreciation of the autobiographical elements in La Porte étroite.)

(3) Romans and Récits

P. Lafille, André Gide romancier (Hachette, 1954) (The most complete study of Gide the novelist. Treats the genesis, the evolution and the techniques of his fictional work)

S. Ullmann, *The Image in the Modern French Novel* (Cambridge Uni. Press, 1960). (Studies the development of Gide's use of imagery throughout his fictional work: *André Walter — Thésée*)

Two excellent analyses of Gide's art in *La Porte étroite*, both in *L'Information Littéraire* (J.-B. Baillière, Paris): — No. 1 (Jan. 1964), pp. 39-45 (M. Lioure, *Le "Journal d'Alissa"*); No. 3 (May 1964), pp. 130-34 (M. Décaudin, *Sur trois récits d'André Gide*)

(4) *Editions of L'Immoraliste and La Porte Etroite*

In *Romans* (Bibl. de la Pléiade, N.R.F., 1958) (contains useful *notices* for *L'Immoraliste* and *La Porte étroite*, and a long list of variants for *L'Immoraliste*.)

L'Immoraliste (*ed.* E. Marks and R. Tedeschi, McMillan, N.Y. 1963). (The only school edition of *L'Immoraliste*, with introduction, notes and vocabulary, which has so far appeared.)

La Porte étroite (*ed.* M. Shackleton, Harrap, 1958) (This school edition offers an excellent introduction to Gide's work and to *La Porte étroite*.)

(5) *Bibliographies*

A. Naville, *Bibliographie des écrits d'André Gide* (Guy Le Prat, 1949)

C. Martin, *Etat présent des études gidiennes (1951-1963)*, *Critique*, 20 (1964), pp. 598-625. (Critical survey of recent work on Gide).

Suggested Approaches to Gide

One can approach Gide's work from many angles. He is more widely known for his fictional work and for his autobiographical writings, and perhaps less so as literary critic and correspondent.

(a) *the novelist:*

There is considerable variety in Gide's fictional work, which ranges from *récits* like *L'Immoraliste* (1902), *La Porte étroite* (1909), *La Symphonie pastorale* (1919), through *soties* like *Les Caves du Vatican* (1914), to his only true novel, *Les Faux-Monnayeurs* (1926).

(b) *the autobiographer:*

Gide's work is one long self-confession and self-revelation. His greatest monument as a writer is undoubtedly his day-by-day account of his personal life, recorded in the famous *Journal* (1889-1949). Equally popular are his memoirs of childhood and early youth, related in *Si le grain ne meurt . . .* (1926).

(c) *the critic:*

Gide is also a sensitive and perceptive critic of literature, as is revealed in many a page of the *Journal* and in critical essays like *Prétextes* (1903) and *Nouveaux Prétextes* (1911). His most important works of criticism are his study of Dostoievsky (1923) and his *Essai sur Montaigne* (1929).

(d) *the correspondent:*

Also valuable, for the light which they throw on the contemporary period of French literature, are the letters written by Gide to important literary figures of his day. Most revealing of these are the *Correspondance* with Francis Jammes (published 1948), with Paul Claudel (1949) and with Paul Valéry (1955).

Turning more specifically to *L'Immoraliste* and *La Porte étroite*, it is suggested that a preliminary reading of the following books should precede a detailed study of the two *récits*. Take them in this order:

(a) *Si le Grain ne meurt . . .* and *Journal (1889-1908)*
   (for the autobiographical background to the two stories)
(b) *Les Cahiers d'André Walter* and *Les Nourritures terrestres* (the two "lyrical" works against which Gide will react by writing two "critical" works, *L'Immoraliste* and *La Porte étroite*)
(c) J. Delay, *La Jeunesse d'André Gide*

and J. Schlumberger, *Madeleine et André Gide*.

(critical and biographical studies, showing further the extent to which the two *récits* are based on Gide's own early life.)

Brief Chronology

The following brief chronology may also be of assistance in fixing those dates in Gide's career which have direct relevance to *L'Immoraliste* and *La Porte étroite* :–

1869   Birth of Gide.

1880   Death of Gide's father—André brought up by mother and her companion, Miss Shackleton.

1883   Beginning of close relationship between André and cousin Madeleine.

1891   Publication of first book: *Les Cahiers d'André Walter*.

1893   Leaves for North Africa with Paul-Albert Laurens. Falls ill with tuberculosis.

1894   Convalescence at Biskra and return to France via Italy.

1895   Death of mother (May) and marriage with Madeleine (October). Honeymoon journey to Switzerland, Italy and Algeria.

1897   Publication of *Les Nourritures terrestres*.

1899–1901   Composition of *L'Immoraliste*.

1902   Publication of *L'Immoraliste*.

1902–04   Period of intense mental *inquiétude*, depression and apathy.

1905–08   Composition of *La Porte étroite*.

1909   Publication of *La Porte étroite*. Gide plays large part in foundation of *Nouvelle Revue Française*, in first numbers of which appears *La Porte étroite*.